Did you know

that the first alarm clock was made in 1350 by German monks who needed to wake up in time for early morning prayers?

that the first windscreen wipers fitted on cars in Britain had to be operated by hand?

that the first sign of trouble from an orang-utan is usually a loud belch?

that the first top hat worn in London caused such a stir that its wearer was arrested for disturbing the peace?

Well, you do now – and this is only the *first* page! With sections on musical firsts, royal firsts, fasionable firsts, animal firsts and many more, and hundreds of first class batty beginnings.

Also available in Knight Books:

How to Halt a Hiccup and other Handy Hints
Mary Danby

The Rainy Day Survival Book
Jeremy Tapscott

The Soaps Quiz Book
Carol Macmillan

Nick Owen's Sports Quiz
Nick Owen and Sandy Ransford

FIRST CLASS
A Book of Batty Beginnings

Alan Brown

Illustrated by Jeremy Tapscott

KNIGHT BOOKS
Hodder and Stoughton

Text copyright © 1991 by Complete Editions

Illustrations copyright © 1991 by Jeremy Tapscott

First published in Great Britain in 1991 by Knight Books

Second impression 1991

British Library CIP data is available on request from the British Library

ISBN 0-340-54715-4

The characters and situations in this book are entirely imaginary and bear no relation to any real person or actual happenings.

The right of Alan Brown to be identified as the author of the text of this work and of Jeremy Tapscott to be identified as the illustrator of this work has been asserted by them in accordance with the Copyright, Designs and Patents Act 1988.

This book is sold subject to the condition that it shall not, by way of trade or otherwise, be lent, re-sold, hired out or otherwise circulated without the publisher's prior consent in any form of binding or cover other than that in which it is published and without a similar condition including this condition being imposed on the subsequent purchaser.

No part of this publication may be reproduced or transmitted in any form or by any means, electronic or mechanical, including photocopying, recording or any information storage or retrieval system, without either the prior permission in writing from the publisher or a licence, permitting restricted copying. In the United Kingdom such licences are issued by the Copyright Licensing Agency, 90 Tottenham Court Road, London W1P 9HE.

Printed and bound in Great Britain for Hodder and Stoughton Children's Books, a division of Hodder and Stoughton Ltd., Mill Road, Dunton Green, Sevenoaks, Kent TN13 2YA (Editorial Office: 47 Bedford Square, London WC1B 3DP) by Clays Ltd., St Ives plc. Photoset by Rowland Phototypesetting Ltd., Bury St Edmunds, Suffolk.

The first successful way of splitting slabs of marble was developed in Ancient Greece – using corks. The corks were wedged into cracks in the marble and then made to expand by being soaked in water. As they expanded, the corks caused the marble to crack neatly along the lines where they were placed.

One of the early Governors of the island of Jamaica, Sir Henry Morgan, had first been a pirate.

The first dinosaur was scientifically described in 1824 as *Megalosaurus bucklandi*, the great fossil lizard, but its remains had first been found even earlier than this, before 1818 by workmen in a slate quarry near Woodstock, Oxford.

The shop sign used by pawnbrokers, who lend money in exchange for goods lodged with them on a temporary basis, is three golden balls. This was first chosen because the balls were part of the coat of arms of the Medici family of Italy, who were extremely powerful money-lenders in Florence in the fourteenth and fifteenth centuries.

The first combs are thought to be those made by the ancient Syrians over 3,000 years ago.

When they were first made, the beautiful white statues of Ancient Greece and Rome were painted with bright colours to show clothing and jewels.

The first bicycle was designed in 1493 by Leonardo da Vinci, the great Italian artist, scientist and inventor. But it was not until 1839 that a bicycle was *built*.

The first gardens in England were made by the Romans in AD 43. The earliest *surviving* garden is at Romsey Abbey in Hampshire and was created in about 1092.

The Ancient Egyptians were the first people to brand their cattle to indicate ownership. Tomb paintings of that period show cattle being branded in almost the same way as it is still done today.

Everest was conquered for the first time on 29 May, 1953.

One of the first things said about chewing-gum was that it would dry up your saliva and stick your stomach together.

The brightly coloured, strong-smelling flowers of the nasturtium first gave the plant its name, based on the Latin *nasus* meaning 'nose' and *tortum* meaning 'to twist'. Translated literally, this name means 'punch-on-the-nose'. Next time you are in a garden where nasturtiums are growing see if the smell of the flowers hits you where it hurts!

The saying 'To keep the wolf from the door' originates from the days when packs of wolves ran wild in the streets of many cities in Europe, terrorising the people who lived there. The people of Paris finally heaved a sigh of relief in 1438 when the last pack of wolves disappeared from their streets.

The first gymnast to be awarded a perfect score of ten in an international competition was Nadia Comaneci of Romania in the 1976 Olympics.

When the story of Cinderella was first told, the heroine wore fur slippers rather than glass ones. The change to the more fairy-tale sounding glass slippers arose through a mistranslation from French, because the French word *verre* for glass is similar to the word *vair* meaning squirrel fur. This probably helped the story to become a perennial favourite.

The first man to climb the famous Matterhorn mountain on the Swiss-Italian border was called Mr Whymper.

Trevor Francis was the first soccer player to be transferred from one club to another for a million pounds. This sum was paid in 1979 when he was transferred from Birmingham to Nottingham Forest.

The idea of freezing food first occurred to a man called Clarence Birdseye. He saw that fish which had been frozen alive in ice for months could swim off unharmed when the ice thawed. As a result he began the company which is famous for its fish fingers.

A man called Nicholas Cugnot has the distinction of being both the first motorist and also the first person to be put in prison for a traffic offence. He drove his steam-powered tractor into a stone wall at a top speed of 6½ kmph (4 mph).

The first people to play with balls made of rubber were the Maya Indians, who lived in Central America nearly 1,000 years ago.

Louis Braille first lost the sight of one eye in an accident in his father's carpentry workshop when he was only three years old, and then found himself totally blind soon afterwards. He began teaching blind people and invented an alphabet of raised letters known as Braille that could be read by touch instead of sight. He died in 1852, little knowing how many millions of blind people would be grateful for his invention.

The first thing that most people think of in association with Eskimos is igloos. But in 1920 a census revealed that less than two per cent of Eskimos had ever seen an igloo, let alone lived in one!

The great artist and inventor Leonardo da Vinci invented the scissors.

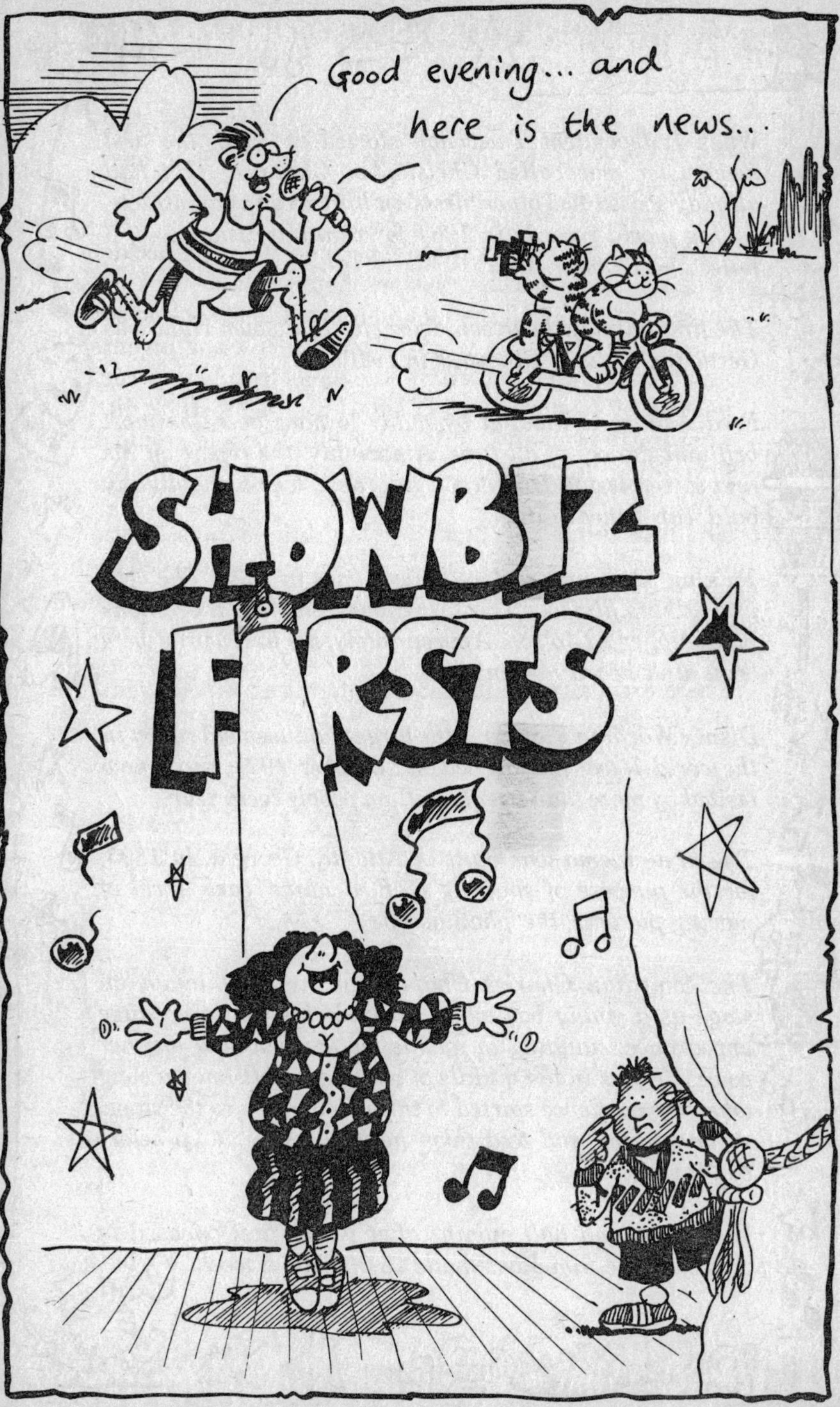
Good evening... and here is the news...
SHOWBIZ FIRSTS

When Independent Television started in 1955, the first newscaster was called Christopher Chataway. He had already scored two other 'firsts' in his career as an athlete, setting world records in 1964 for running distances of 3 miles and 5,000 metres.

The first animated cartoon character in its own right was Gertie the Trained Dinosaur in 1910.

Fred Astaire is thought by many to have been the most brilliant dancer of all time. Amazingly, the report on his first screen test in Hollywood recorded: 'Can't act, slightly bald, can dance a little'.

Talking films first replaced silent ones in 1928. The very first talking film was The Jazz Singer, starring the famous black singer Al Jolson. Appropriately, his first words were 'You ain't heard nothing yet.'

Disney World in Florida is the largest amusement resort in the world. It was first opened on 1 October, 1971, and is now visited by more than twenty million people every year.

The first cinema was built in Atlanta, Georgia, in 1895, for the purpose of showing C. F. Jenkins' early form of moving pictures, the 'phantascope'.

The comedian Charles Chaplin got his first laugh on stage as a young boy when he made his first ever stage appearance, standing in for his mother who had lost her voice. He was in the middle of singing a well-known song when the audience started to throw money on to the stage, so he stopped and told them he would pick it up before continuing.

In the two and half months after it was first released in America, the film Jaws made £5,000,000 a week.

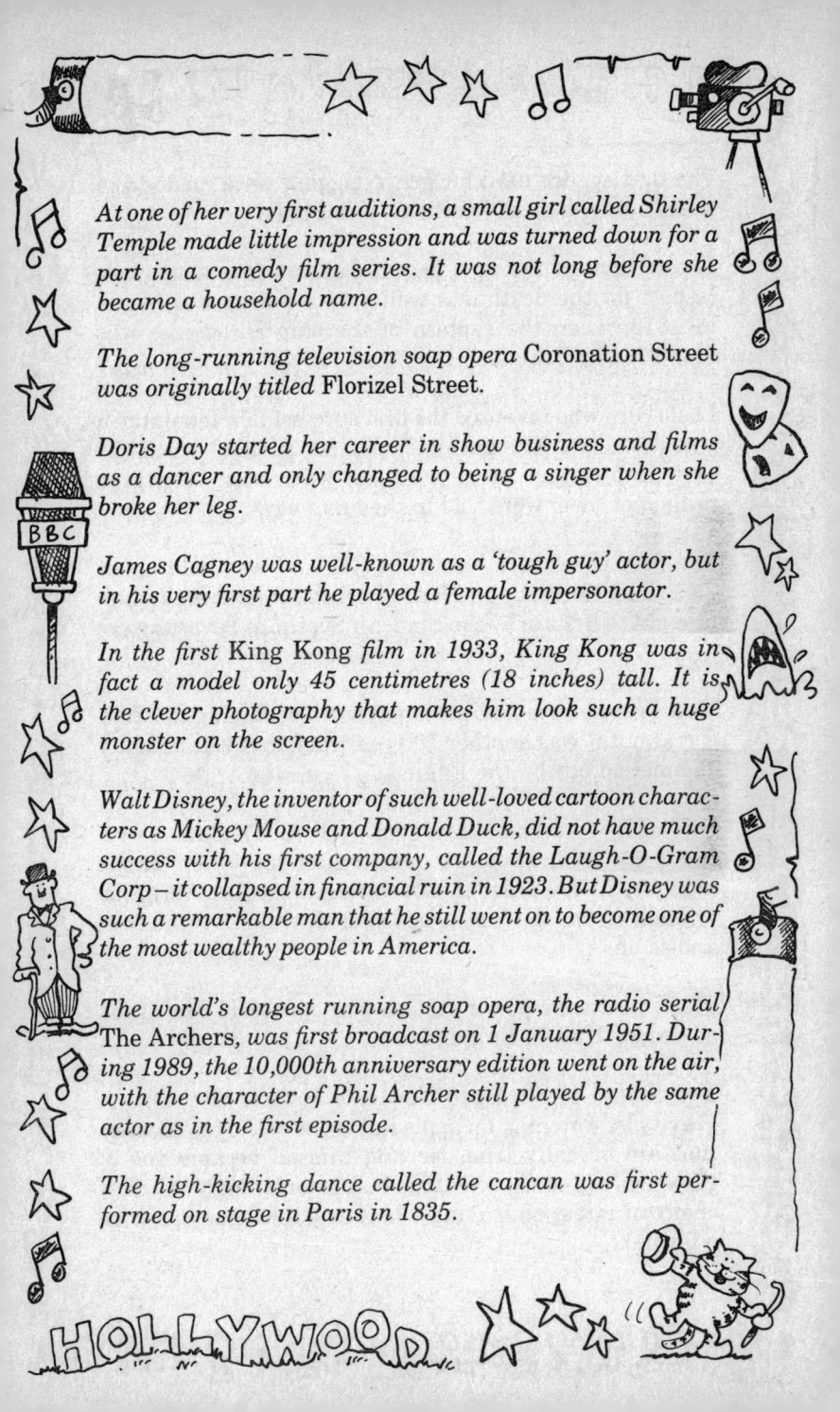

At one of her very first auditions, a small girl called Shirley Temple made little impression and was turned down for a part in a comedy film series. It was not long before she became a household name.

The long-running television soap opera Coronation Street was originally titled Florizel Street.

Doris Day started her career in show business and films as a dancer and only changed to being a singer when she broke her leg.

James Cagney was well-known as a 'tough guy' actor, but in his very first part he played a female impersonator.

In the first King Kong film in 1933, King Kong was in fact a model only 45 centimetres (18 inches) tall. It is the clever photography that makes him look such a huge monster on the screen.

Walt Disney, the inventor of such well-loved cartoon characters as Mickey Mouse and Donald Duck, did not have much success with his first company, called the Laugh-O-Gram Corp – it collapsed in financial ruin in 1923. But Disney was such a remarkable man that he still went on to become one of the most wealthy people in America.

The world's longest running soap opera, the radio serial The Archers, was first broadcast on 1 January 1951. During 1989, the 10,000th anniversary edition went on the air, with the character of Phil Archer still played by the same actor as in the first episode.

The high-kicking dance called the cancan was first performed on stage in Paris in 1835.

The first spades used for grave-digging were made from the shoulder bones of prehistoric animals.

The custom of flying a flag at half-mast as a mark of respect for the death of a well-known person was begun in 1612, when the captain of the ship *Heartsease* was murdered by Eskimos.

Laslo Biro who invented the first successful ball-point pen was actually a Hungarian hypnotist. In 1959 when the first throw-away biros went on sale, over fifty-three million of them were sold in the first year.

The first horse race known in England was held about AD 210 at Netherby in North Yorkshire. Arabian horses brought to Britain by the Emperor Septimus Severus were used.

Napoleon was the first person to think of digging the Suez Canal but it was another 100 years before it was actually channelled out by the English.

Vitamins were first discovered by F. G. Hopkins as recently as 1907. They are named after the letters of the alphabet in the order in which they were discovered, so vitamin A was the first to be isolated, vitamin B the next and so on.

The first atomic power station was opened in May 1957 at Calder Hall in England.

The legend of Sir Isaac Newton's historic discovery of gravity by watching an apple fall is one of the few legends that are actually true. Newton himself became one of the world's greatest scientists but, astonishingly, his first choice of career on leaving school as a teenager was to be a farmer.

The word 'trillion' was first used in 1484.

The Egyptians were the first people to use wedding rings. In their form of 'written' or picture language, called hieroglyphics, the ring shape meant eternity. The custom of wearing a wedding ring on the third finger of the left hand was begun by the Romans who believed there was a nerve going direct from the heart to this finger.

Food was first eaten off plates in the fifteenth century. Until this time people made do with a thick slice of bread to put their food on at the table.

It was the famous naturalist Charles Darwin who first came up with the theory that all animals evolve or develop from other animals and that man had evolved from apes. When his book *The Origin of Species*, which outlined his ideas, was first published he thought that the 1,250 copies of it that were printed would be too many to sell. In fact, all the copies sold on the first day of publication.

The magic word *Abracadabra* was first used as a charm against hay fever.

'Lead' pencils have never been made with lead; even the first ones were made with graphite.

The first UK Snooker Championship was held at Blackpool Tower Circus in 1977. It was won by the Irishman Patsy Fagan.

When Kodak hand-held cameras were first used, people had to send the whole camera in for processing, in order to get the film developed into photographs.

Tea bags were invented by mistake! A tea merchant wrapped up some samples of tea in cloth for customers to try, but they did not realise they were meant to open the bags to use the tea and so the idea of tea bags was born.

Slot machines have been around longer than you may think! They were first used in ancient temples in the town of Alexandria as early as 641 BC. In this instance, a coin could buy some holy water which was used by the worshipper as an offering.

Although gold is one of the rarest metals, it was the first to be discovered.

The first ever fan club was called, rather oddly, 'The Keen Order of Wallerites'. Members were fans of the popular actor-manager, Lewis Waller.

The patron saint of England is St George, who actually originated in the Middle East when the Knights of the Crusades spread his fame throughout Europe. The story goes that he went to their aid when fighting the battle of Antioch in 1089.

Rowan trees were first planted in churchyards because they were thought to keep the powers of witchcraft away from the dead.

The origin of the practice of having a twenty-one gun salute at military burials and ringing church bells at Christian funerals dates back to the pagan custom of making as much noise as possible to ward off evil spirits when someone dies.

The great tennis player Fred Perry was the first person to win all four of the major singles titles – Australia, France, Wimbledon and the United States. But he never held all four titles at the same time and therefore did not achieve the so-called Grand Slam.

The custom of serving fish with a slice of lemon has its origin in the Middle Ages when people believed that the juice of lemons could dissolve fish bones swallowed by mistake. Nowadays, lemon is believed to improve the flavour of fish, so the custom is still widespread although the reason for doing it has changed.

Los Angeles was first given the name El Pueblo de Nuestra Senora la Reina de los Angeles de Porciuncula. No wonder it was renamed Los Angeles!

An eleven-year-old British girl called Donna Griffiths first began sneezing continuously in January 1981 and did not stop until 16 September, 1983 – the 978th day. She sneezed an estimated million times in the first 365 days.

A man called Henry Burling was the first person to settle in Featherston, New Zealand. When he died at the age of 110, he left 600 descendants.

The first fig trees were cultivated in Egypt in 4,000 BC.

In the 1956 British Marbles Championships, a team called the Toucan Terribles won the first of their twenty consecutive titles.

The phrase 'nosey parker' used to describe someone who is always interfering was first applied to Matthew Parker, who was Archbishop of Canterbury during the reign of Queen Elizabeth I.

Graham Gooch was the first batsman to score a century for England in a one-day international cricket match. He hit his runs against the West Indies in Trinidad in 1986, in a match in which England won on the last ball.

The first person to make horses dance to music at parades was a cavalry officer of the Sybarite army (the Sybarites lived in Ancient Greece between 720 and 510 BC). This idea was very popular until the cavalry charged a nearby town and tried to conquer it. The people in the town knew about the horses and played music on their pipes to make them dance. As a result the whole army was very quickly defeated and the cavalry officer became very unpopular.

Aesop, the writer of the well-known fables, was a Greek slave in the first place, but his talent for telling stories won him his freedom and later fame.

The first mechanically frozen ice rink was opened in 1876. It was situated near the King's Road in London and was called The Glaciarium.

The first encyclopaedia of proven existence was published in 1559 and was written by Paul Scalich. The Chinese are said to have compiled an encyclopaedia even before the birth of Christ, but no evidence of it has survived although there are said to have been three huge copies. The word 'encyclopaedia' actually means 'learning within a circle'.

When television was first invented, a contributor to the *Listener* magazine wrote: 'It won't last, it's a flash in the pan.'

Sir Robert Walpole became Britain's first Prime Minister in 1721 at the comparatively young age of forty-five.

The idea of making paper from wood was first perceived by the French scientist René de Réaumur in the early 1700s, when he watched wasps making their papery nests by chewing up wood and then using the resulting saliva-mixed pulp to build the nest.

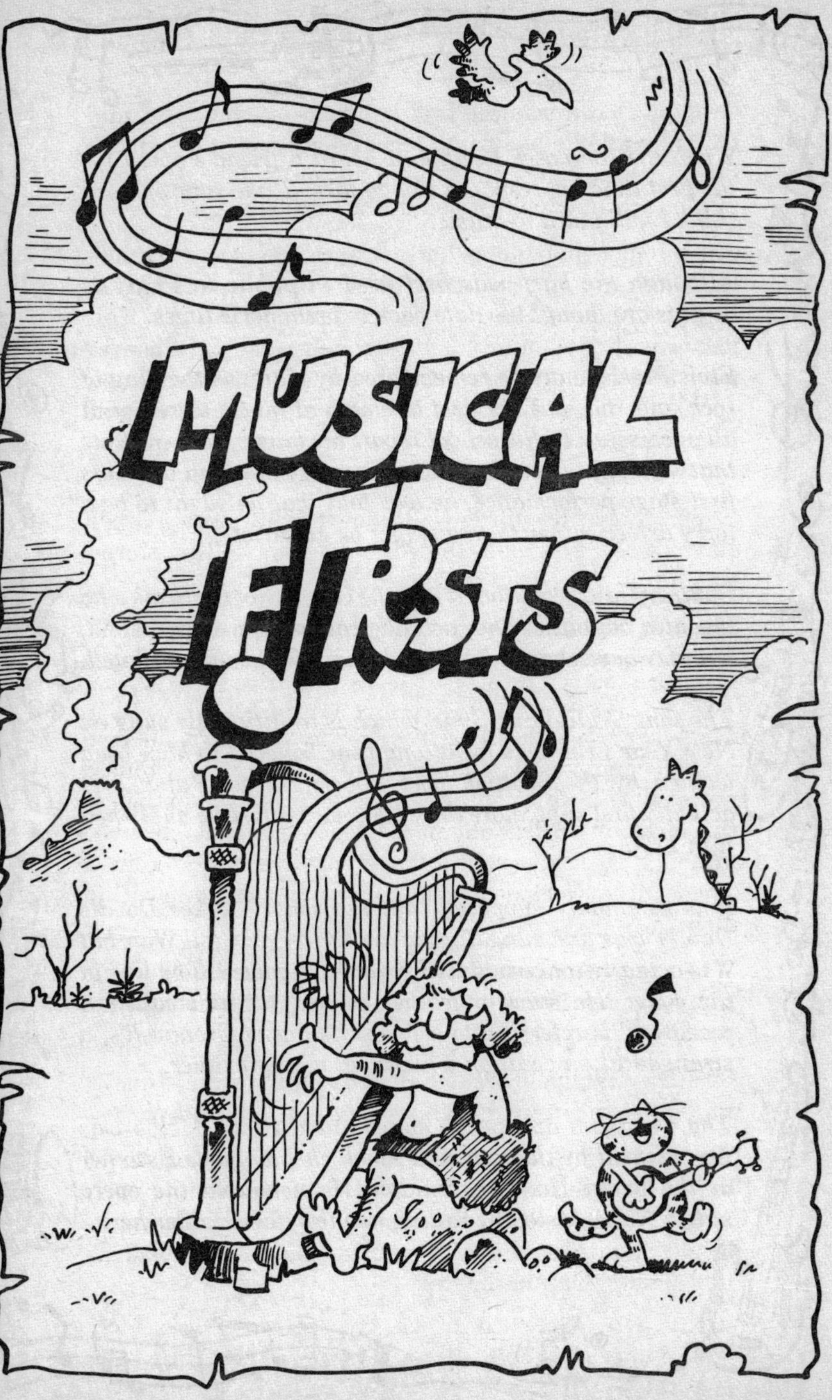
MUSICAL FIRSTS

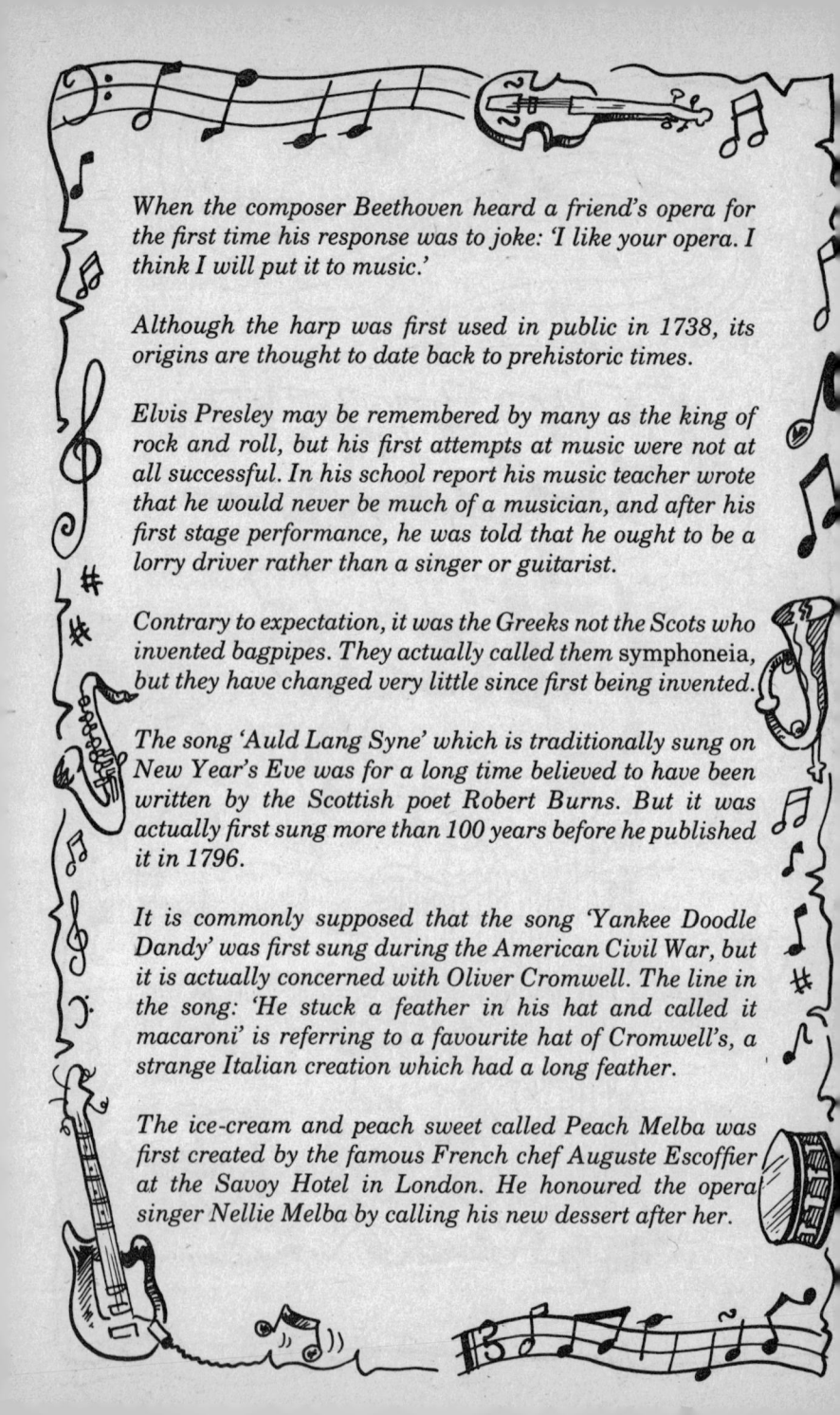

When the composer Beethoven heard a friend's opera for the first time his response was to joke: 'I like your opera. I think I will put it to music.'

Although the harp was first used in public in 1738, its origins are thought to date back to prehistoric times.

Elvis Presley may be remembered by many as the king of rock and roll, but his first attempts at music were not at all successful. In his school report his music teacher wrote that he would never be much of a musician, and after his first stage performance, he was told that he ought to be a lorry driver rather than a singer or guitarist.

Contrary to expectation, it was the Greeks not the Scots who invented bagpipes. They actually called them symphoneia, *but they have changed very little since first being invented.*

The song 'Auld Lang Syne' which is traditionally sung on New Year's Eve was for a long time believed to have been written by the Scottish poet Robert Burns. But it was actually first sung more than 100 years before he published it in 1796.

It is commonly supposed that the song 'Yankee Doodle Dandy' was first sung during the American Civil War, but it is actually concerned with Oliver Cromwell. The line in the song: 'He stuck a feather in his hat and called it macaroni' is referring to a favourite hat of Cromwell's, a strange Italian creation which had a long feather.

The ice-cream and peach sweet called Peach Melba was first created by the famous French chef Auguste Escoffier at the Savoy Hotel in London. He honoured the opera singer Nellie Melba by calling his new dessert after her.

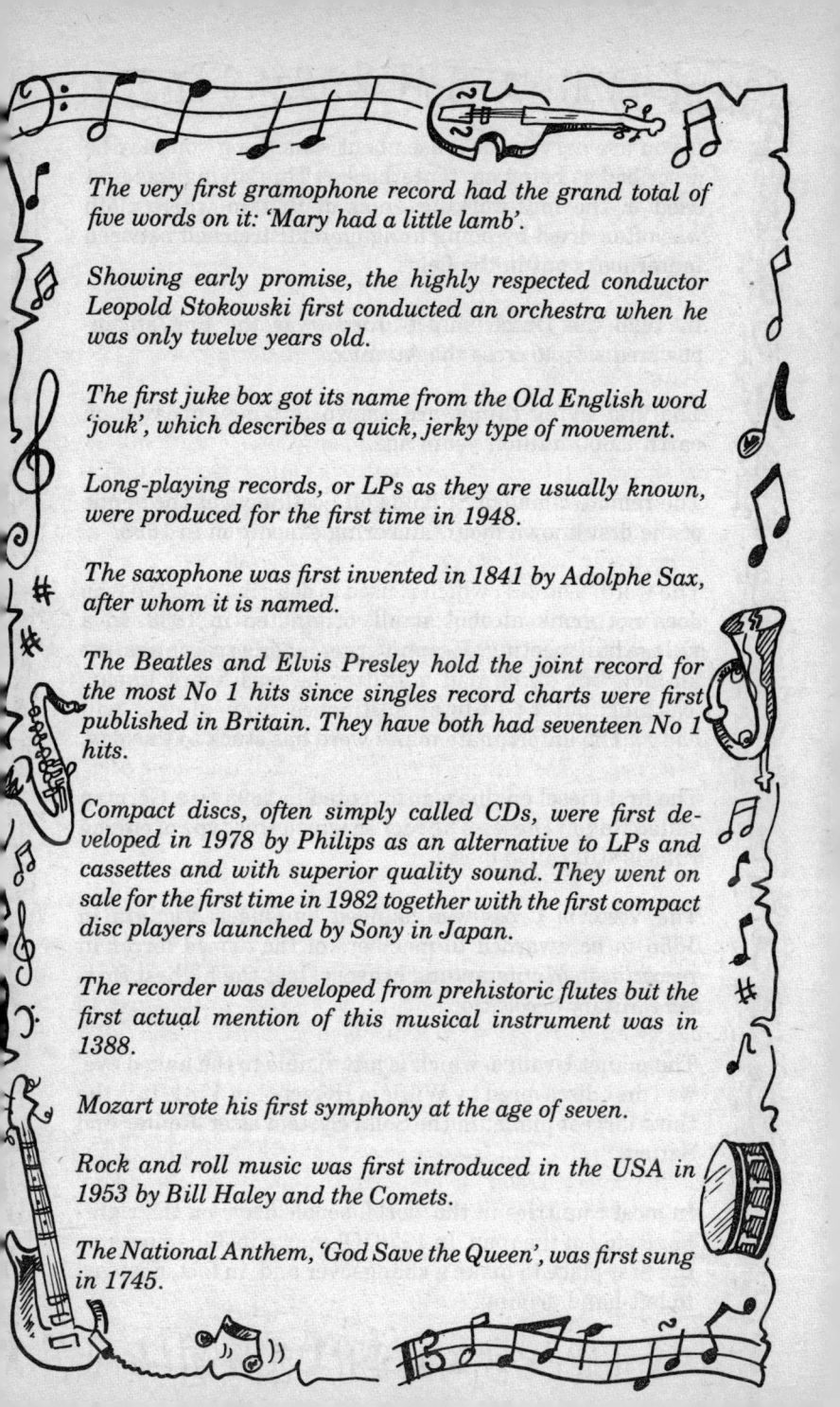

The very first gramophone record had the grand total of five words on it: 'Mary had a little lamb'.

Showing early promise, the highly respected conductor Leopold Stokowski first conducted an orchestra when he was only twelve years old.

The first juke box got its name from the Old English word 'jouk', which describes a quick, jerky type of movement.

Long-playing records, or LPs as they are usually known, were produced for the first time in 1948.

The saxophone was first invented in 1841 by Adolphe Sax, after whom it is named.

The Beatles and Elvis Presley hold the joint record for the most No 1 hits since singles record charts were first published in Britain. They have both had seventeen No 1 hits.

Compact discs, often simply called CDs, were first developed in 1978 by Philips as an alternative to LPs and cassettes and with superior quality sound. They went on sale for the first time in 1982 together with the first compact disc players launched by Sony in Japan.

The recorder was developed from prehistoric flutes but the first actual mention of this musical instrument was in 1388.

Mozart wrote his first symphony at the age of seven.

Rock and roll music was first introduced in the USA in 1953 by Bill Haley and the Comets.

The National Anthem, 'God Save the Queen', was first sung in 1745.

If you are nervous or tense about something you may be described as being on 'tenterhooks'. This saying was first used in the mill-working areas of Britain where cloth was often dried by being hung on and stretched between tenterhooks out in the fields.

In 1826 the Dutch ship *Curaçao* was the first steam-powered ship to cross the Atlantic.

The first living things are known to have appeared on earth 2,000 million years ago.

The remote island of St Kilda off Scotland was the venue of the first known mountaineering expedition in 1698.

The word 'teetotal', which is used to describe a person who does not drink alcohol at all, originated in 1833. In a village hall meeting, Joseph Turner made a speech against alcohol, but as he had a stutter he was heard to say: 'Nothing but t-t-t-t-total abstinence from alcohol will do . . .' The unfortunate man's word has stuck to this day.

The first diesel engine was invented in 1895 by a German called Rudolf Diesel. The fuel on which this type of engine runs is still called diesel.

The Victoria Cross was founded by Queen Victoria in 1856 to be awarded to members of the armed forces in recognition of outstanding bravery. It is the highest British military decoration.

The planet Uranus, which is just visible to the naked eye, was first discovered by William Herschel in 1781. It is the third largest planet in the Solar System after Jupiter and Saturn.

In most countries in the world, people drive on the right-hand side of the road. In 1978, Okinawa in Japan became the first place to make a changeover and, in fact, changed to left-hand driving.

The introduction of tea, coffee and cocoa from the East led to the opening of the first coffee houses in seventeenth-century England. They were places in which men could meet to discuss business and smoke their clay pipes.

A form of the vaulting horse used by modern gymnasts was first used in the days of the Roman Empire by cavalrymen, who used a wooden horse to practise jumping in and out of the saddle.

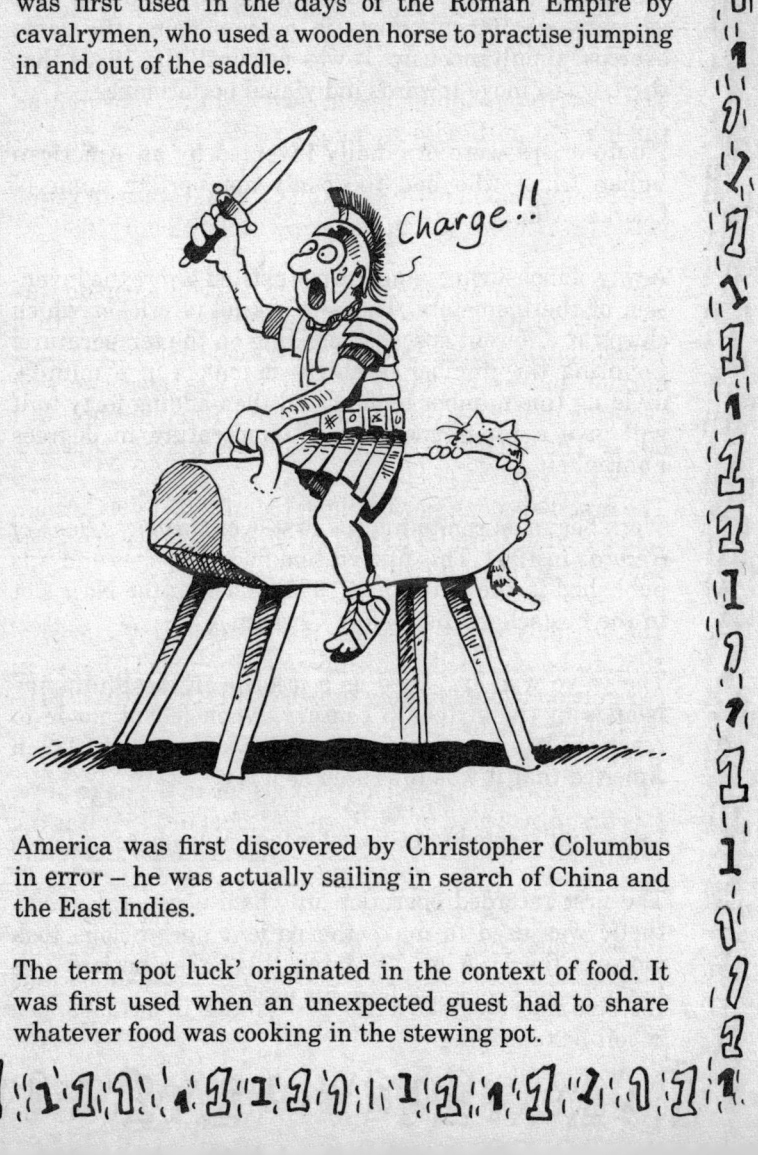

America was first discovered by Christopher Columbus in error – he was actually sailing in search of China and the East Indies.

The term 'pot luck' originated in the context of food. It was first used when an unexpected guest had to share whatever food was cooking in the stewing pot.

The first bricks used in building are reckoned to be more than 10,000 years old. The ancient city of Babylon was built with walls of brick 26 metres thick.

When gymnastics first became part of the Olympic Games, the floor exercises were usually mass performances with as many as 100 gymnasts in a team doing the same exercise simultaneously. It was not until the 1930s that there was a move towards individual performance.

Potato crisps were originally invented by an American Indian Chief who had the oddly appropriate name of George Crum.

A way of measuring temperature existed *before* the invention of thermometers. There is a kind of cricket which chirps at different speeds depending on the temperature. Counting the number of chirps it makes in a minute, dividing this number by four and then adding forty to it will give a rough measure of temperature in degrees Fahrenheit.

Work began on compiling the first ever *Guinness Book of Records* in 1954. This first edition had 198 pages and was published in the autumn of 1955, reaching the No 1 slot in the bestsellers' list before Christmas.

The yo-yo was first used as a *weapon* in the Philippine Islands in the sixteenth century, when it was made to reach out to a length of 7 metres. It was not until 1929 in America that it was first used as a toy.

Laces first started to be used for fastening shoes in 1790.

The first recorded operation in which a general anaesthetic was used to make the patient unconscious took place in the USA on 30 March, 1842. The patient was having a cyst removed from his neck.

Hearing a male cuckoo's call, usually in the first weeks of April in southern Britain, is regarded as a sign that spring has arrived. But the earliest day in the year on which a cuckoo has first been reliably recorded as being heard and seen in Britain is 2 March. This was recorded in Oxfordshire in 1972.

Teddy bears were first named after the American President, Theodore (Teddy) Roosevelt. The President was on one occasion photographed with a baby bear, which resulted in stuffed toy bears or 'teddy' bears becoming popular. They have remained a universal favourite ever since.

The first hard hats were worn in 1585 by workers involved in building the Vatican, the Pope's residence in Rome.

There is a strange way of greeting guests in Tibet. When visitors first arrive at a house, they are welcomed by everyone sticking out their tongues.

The world's first hydrogen balloon was launched in Paris in 1783. It landed in a field 24 kilometres away, where farmers thought it must either be an evil spirit or a piece of the moon and so ripped it into little pieces.

Chinese and Japanese babies have a blue mark on their bottoms for the first two years of their lives.

Pablo Picasso was a very famous painter, but his full name is not so well known. It was Pablo Diego José Francisco de Paula Juan Nepomuceno Maria de los Remedios Cipriano de la Santissima Trinidad Ruiz Picasso.

Table tennis or ping-pong was invented by James Gibb in 1926, but it was first called 'Gossamer'.

The Salvation Army was founded by William Booth, an English preacher, in the nineteenth century. Uniforms were first worn in 1880, including the distinctive bonnet chosen by Catherine Booth.

Education first became compulsory in England in 1870, for children from five to twelve years old. Before this, many children did not learn to read or write at all.

The first foam rubber, like so many inventions, was created accidentally. No one knows why, but someone put some latex or natural rubber into a food mixer. When the mixer was switched on the rubber was whipped up into a foam.

Denmark was the first country to have its own national flag. The design of a white cross on a red background was created in 1219.

The Peruvians were making and using instant mashed potato hundreds of years ago, long before it was known in Europe. They discovered that by leaving potatoes in the ground to freeze, they could then grind them up into a powder which they could store for a long time. When they wanted to use the potato they simply mixed it with water to make a sort of mash.

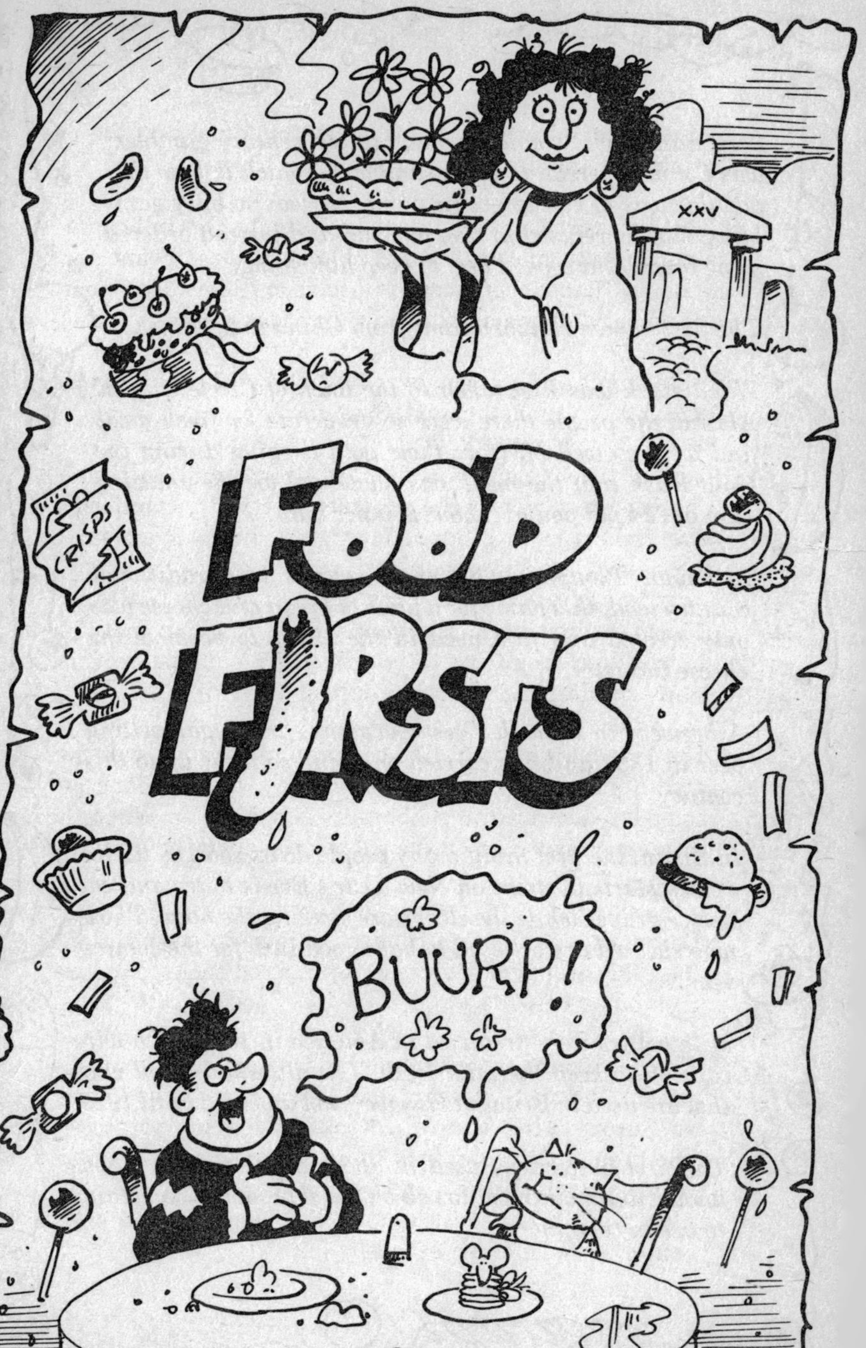

XXV
CRISPS
FOOD FIRSTS
BUURP!

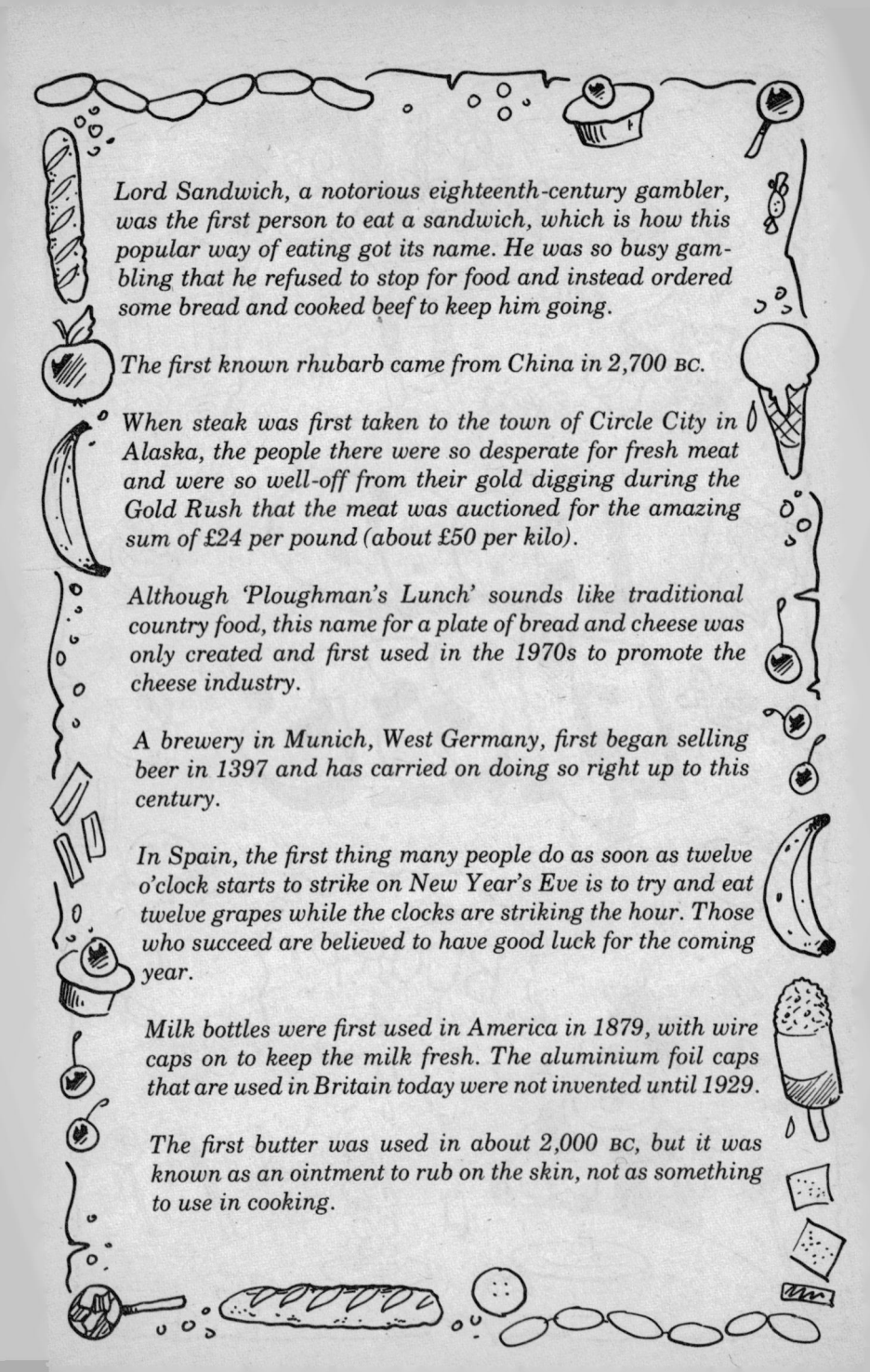

Lord Sandwich, a notorious eighteenth-century gambler, was the first person to eat a sandwich, which is how this popular way of eating got its name. He was so busy gambling that he refused to stop for food and instead ordered some bread and cooked beef to keep him going.

The first known rhubarb came from China in 2,700 BC.

When steak was first taken to the town of Circle City in Alaska, the people there were so desperate for fresh meat and were so well-off from their gold digging during the Gold Rush that the meat was auctioned for the amazing sum of £24 per pound (about £50 per kilo).

Although 'Ploughman's Lunch' sounds like traditional country food, this name for a plate of bread and cheese was only created and first used in the 1970s to promote the cheese industry.

A brewery in Munich, West Germany, first began selling beer in 1397 and has carried on doing so right up to this century.

In Spain, the first thing many people do as soon as twelve o'clock starts to strike on New Year's Eve is to try and eat twelve grapes while the clocks are striking the hour. Those who succeed are believed to have good luck for the coming year.

Milk bottles were first used in America in 1879, with wire caps on to keep the milk fresh. The aluminium foil caps that are used in Britain today were not invented until 1929.

The first butter was used in about 2,000 BC, but it was known as an ointment to rub on the skin, not as something to use in cooking.

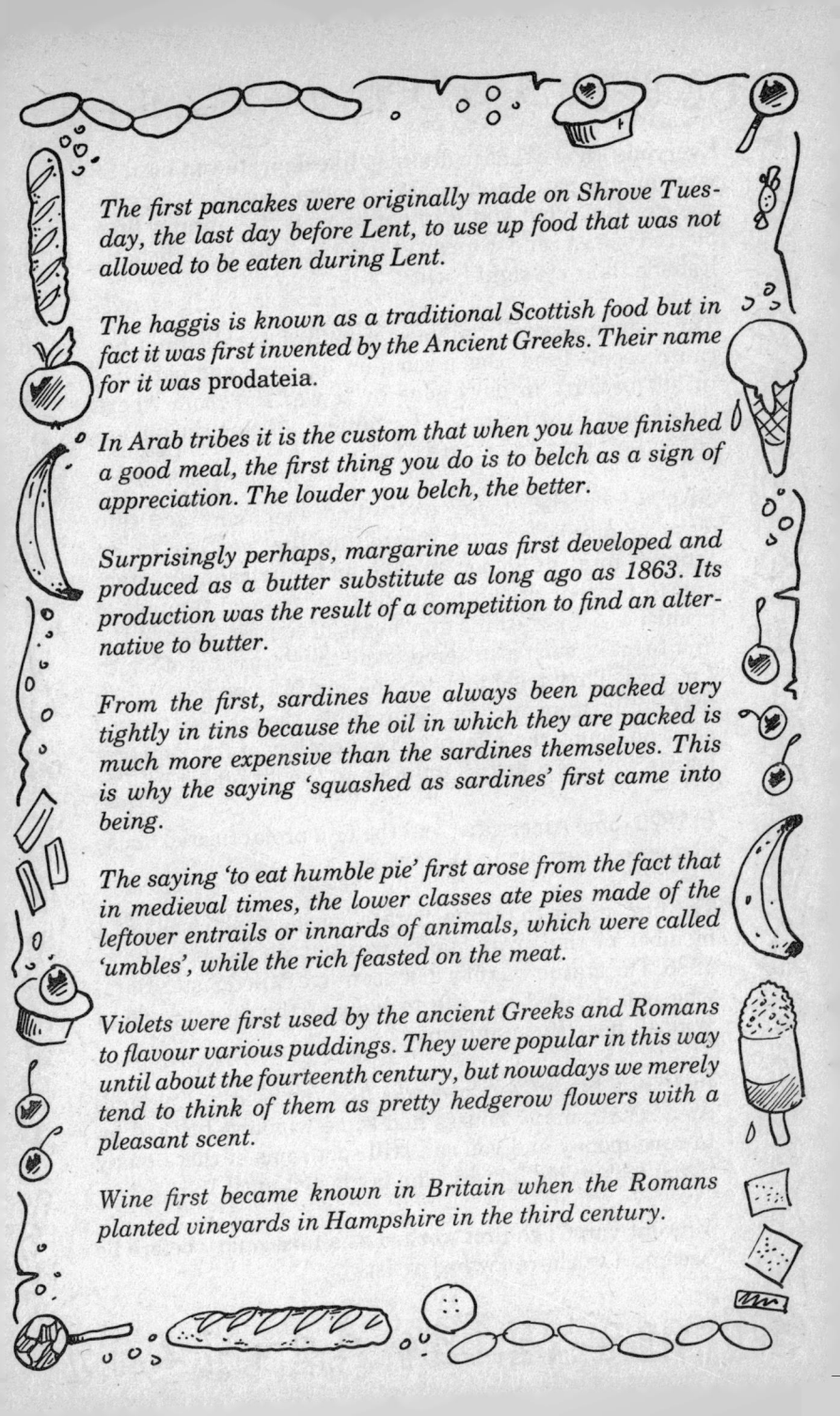

The first pancakes were originally made on Shrove Tuesday, the last day before Lent, to use up food that was not allowed to be eaten during Lent.

The haggis is known as a traditional Scottish food but in fact it was first invented by the Ancient Greeks. Their name for it was prodateia.

In Arab tribes it is the custom that when you have finished a good meal, the first thing you do is to belch as a sign of appreciation. The louder you belch, the better.

Surprisingly perhaps, margarine was first developed and produced as a butter substitute as long ago as 1863. Its production was the result of a competition to find an alternative to butter.

From the first, sardines have always been packed very tightly in tins because the oil in which they are packed is much more expensive than the sardines themselves. This is why the saying 'squashed as sardines' first came into being.

The saying 'to eat humble pie' first arose from the fact that in medieval times, the lower classes ate pies made of the leftover entrails or innards of animals, which were called 'umbles', while the rich feasted on the meat.

Violets were first used by the ancient Greeks and Romans to flavour various puddings. They were popular in this way until about the fourteenth century, but nowadays we merely tend to think of them as pretty hedgerow flowers with a pleasant scent.

Wine first became known in Britain when the Romans planted vineyards in Hampshire in the third century.

Everyone knows that to dress up like a pirate you need to wear an eye patch and to have a large hooped earring in one ear. But what you may not know is that pirates first pierced one ear and wore an earring because they thought it made their eyesight better!

The drawing-room in a house was first so-called not because people used it as a room for drawing and painting in but because in days gone by it was the room where ladies used to 'withdraw' after dinner, leaving the men to enjoy their port and cigars.

Just as scientists today try to find ever more accurate ways of predicting and controlling the weather in an attempt to avoid major tornado and hurricane disasters and to prevent droughts causing widespread famine, so primitive man tried his own forms of control. Among the first to make such an attempt were the Peruvians of South America. They tried to catch the sun in huge nets which they hung from towers. Improbable though this seems now, no doubt the efforts of twentieth-century meteorologists will seem just as unlikely in the far-off future.

In 1820 some Americans sent the first prefabricated house to missionaries living in Hawaii.

The first statue to commemorate a woman who was not a member of the royal family was put up as recently as 1886. The statue was of a district nurse called Sister Dora, who had devoted her life to helping the poor people of Walsall near Birmingham.

In 1696 a tax on windows was first imposed in England. As a result, many houses had some windows bricked up to save money and you can still spot some of these today if you look at old houses. The tax lasted until 1851.

Vincent van Gogh first worked as a missionary before he became a world-renowned artist.

The first recorded eclipse of the sun was the cause of death of a group of Chinese astronomers. The astronomers had been told to calculate when the eclipse would take place, but they failed to predict it accurately and were all executed as a result.

The first spectacles were probably those worn by Italians in 1289, which were used to help weak eyesight. The first individual spectacles were not developed until 1623, by which time lenses of different powers could be made to suit people with different eyesight problems.

The idea of giving a small sum of money called a 'tip' to someone who has offered a good or satisfactory service, first began in pubs. In the seventeenth century the words 'To Insure Promptness' were often displayed to customers and it is from the initials of this phrase that the word 'tip' originates.

The first letter of the alphabet, 'A', is also the name of a town in Sweden.

Stone tools were first made about two and a half million years ago by prehistoric men.

In 1929 the *Graf Zeppelin* made history by becoming the first airship to fly round the world. It took 21 days, 7½ hours to complete its voyage.

The first camel-hair painters' brushes were given the name because they were made by a man called Camel, not because they were made of camel's hair. Camel-hair brushes are made from the tail hairs of squirrels.

The uniforms worn by the famous Swiss Guards at the Vatican, the Pope's residence in Rome, were first designed in the 1500s by the great painter Michelangelo. The design has not changed since they were first worn 450 years ago – except for the addition of tear-gas grenades in 1975.

The first guns took so long to load and fire that bows and arrows were about twelve times more efficient.

The first council houses were built in ancient Rome after the city's population had increased dramatically for three consecutive years.

The 'talkies', or first cinema films with speech, put a premature end to the careers of a number of film stars. One such star of silent films was John Gilbert, whose masculine reputation was cruelly shattered when the public heard his rather squeaky voice for the first time. He made his last film, *The Captain Hates the Sea*, in 1934.

Farthings, which were worth a quarter of an old penny, first came into use in Britain in 1279. They continued to be legal tender until 1 January, 1961.

In 1849 Venice was attacked by the Austrians who sent over hot-air balloons carrying fused bombs, thus making it the first city to have bombs dropped upon it from the air.

Sir Edwin Landseer, the Victorian artist, was first responsible for the myth that St Bernard dogs, which are trained to rescue mountaineers, carry casks of brandy around their necks. He painted a St Bernard with a barrel hanging around its neck and this idea was copied in hundreds of other pictures. But in reality this has never been the case.

The first advertisement for Ever Ready batteries stated that they were safe enough to turn on inside a barrel of gunpowder without any reaction!

The names of many English towns and cities originate from Roman times. The Roman word for camp was *castra* and if you look at a map you will see that many place names have 'chester', 'caster' or 'cester' in them, for example, Manchester, Doncaster, Gloucester and Winchester.

In the game of chess, the number of variations in the first four moves alone is 318,979,564,000.

Big Ben in the Houses of Parliament is a world famous London landmark, but the name belongs to the bell *inside* the clock tower rather than the building itself. The bell was first called Big Ben after an eighteenth-century politician called Ben Hall who weighed a massive 158 kilograms.

Avocados are thought to have first grown in Central and South America. Although they are often called avocado pears they are not a type of pear, but are just shaped rather like a pear. Avocados are the most fattening of all the fruits, containing 163 calories per 100 grams.

Jimmy Carter was the first President of the United States to have been born in a hospital. All those before him had been born at home.

In 1872 frozen Australian beef was eaten in England for the first time.

The idea of having a 'best man' at weddings first started in ancient times when bridegrooms took a strong man along with them to help carry off their chosen bride. Nowadays, the best man only carries the wedding ring!

The first ever feature film was, surprisingly, not American but Australian. It was an Australian 'western' called *The Story of the Kelly Gang*.

In 1877 a society was first set up in Belgium with the extraordinary aim of improving the 'morals of domestic cats'.

Austria was the country that issued the first postcards in 1869, followed by Britain in 1872. Postcard collecting has become a widespread hobby since then and is now claimed to come next in popularity after stamp and coin collecting.

The game of billiards first became popular when King Louis XIV of France began playing because his doctors had advised him that his digestion would be improved by the gentle exercise of stretching across the billiards table.

The first atomic bomb to be used in warfare was 10 feet (3.04 metres) long and weighed 9,000 pounds (4,080 kilograms). It was dropped on Hiroshima, Japan, by the United States on 6 August, 1945, with resultant huge devastation and loss of life.

In the Kanga school in India, apprentice miniature-painters are only allowed to paint with a brush for the first time after ten years of training. Some of the brushes they use are so fine that they are made of only one hair.

MEDICAL FIRSTS

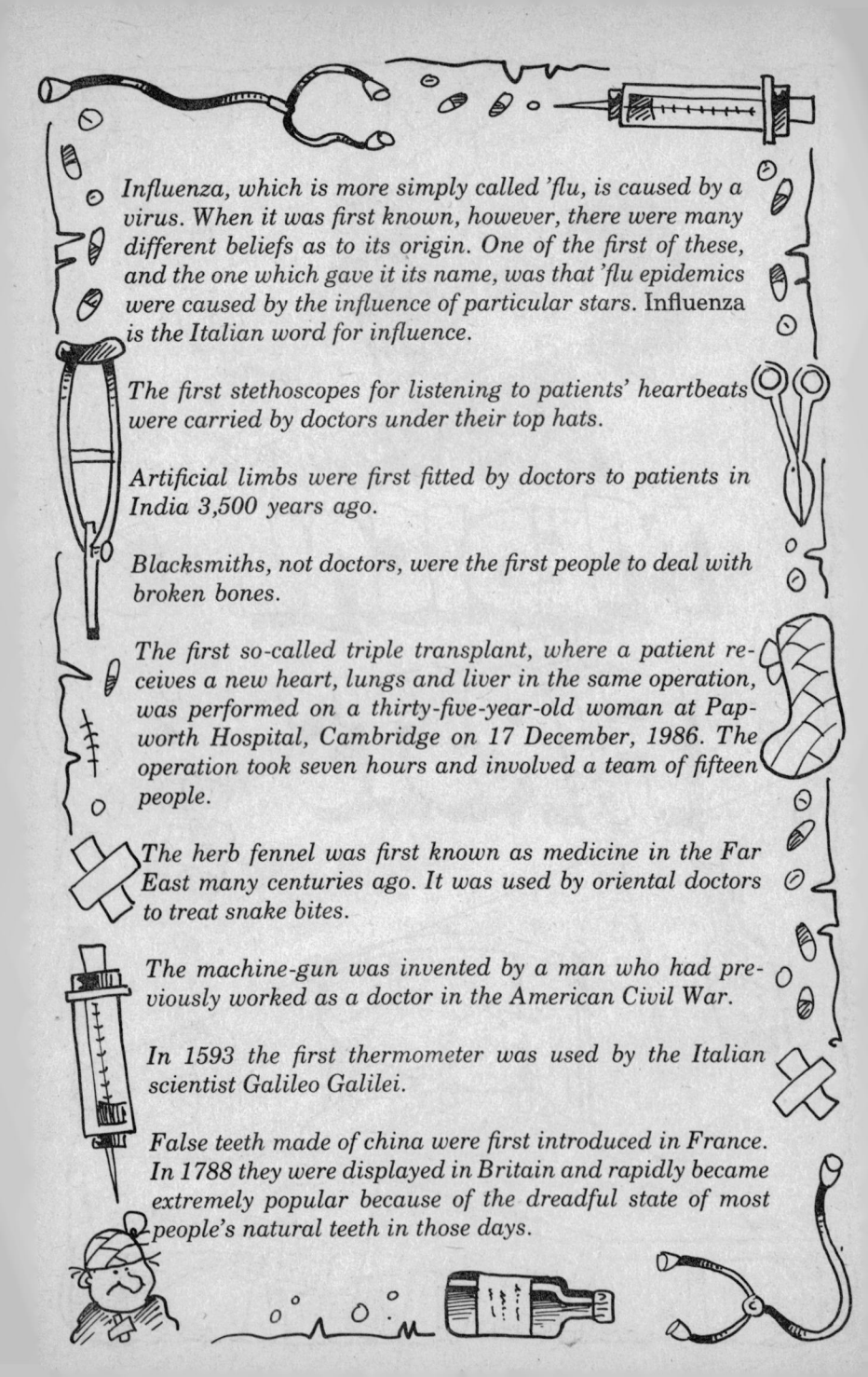

Influenza, which is more simply called 'flu, is caused by a virus. When it was first known, however, there were many different beliefs as to its origin. One of the first of these, and the one which gave it its name, was that 'flu epidemics were caused by the influence of particular stars. Influenza is the Italian word for influence.

The first stethoscopes for listening to patients' heartbeats were carried by doctors under their top hats.

Artificial limbs were first fitted by doctors to patients in India 3,500 years ago.

Blacksmiths, not doctors, were the first people to deal with broken bones.

The first so-called triple transplant, where a patient receives a new heart, lungs and liver in the same operation, was performed on a thirty-five-year-old woman at Papworth Hospital, Cambridge on 17 December, 1986. The operation took seven hours and involved a team of fifteen people.

The herb fennel was first known as medicine in the Far East many centuries ago. It was used by oriental doctors to treat snake bites.

The machine-gun was invented by a man who had previously worked as a doctor in the American Civil War.

In 1593 the first thermometer was used by the Italian scientist Galileo Galilei.

False teeth made of china were first introduced in France. In 1788 they were displayed in Britain and rapidly became extremely popular because of the dreadful state of most people's natural teeth in those days.

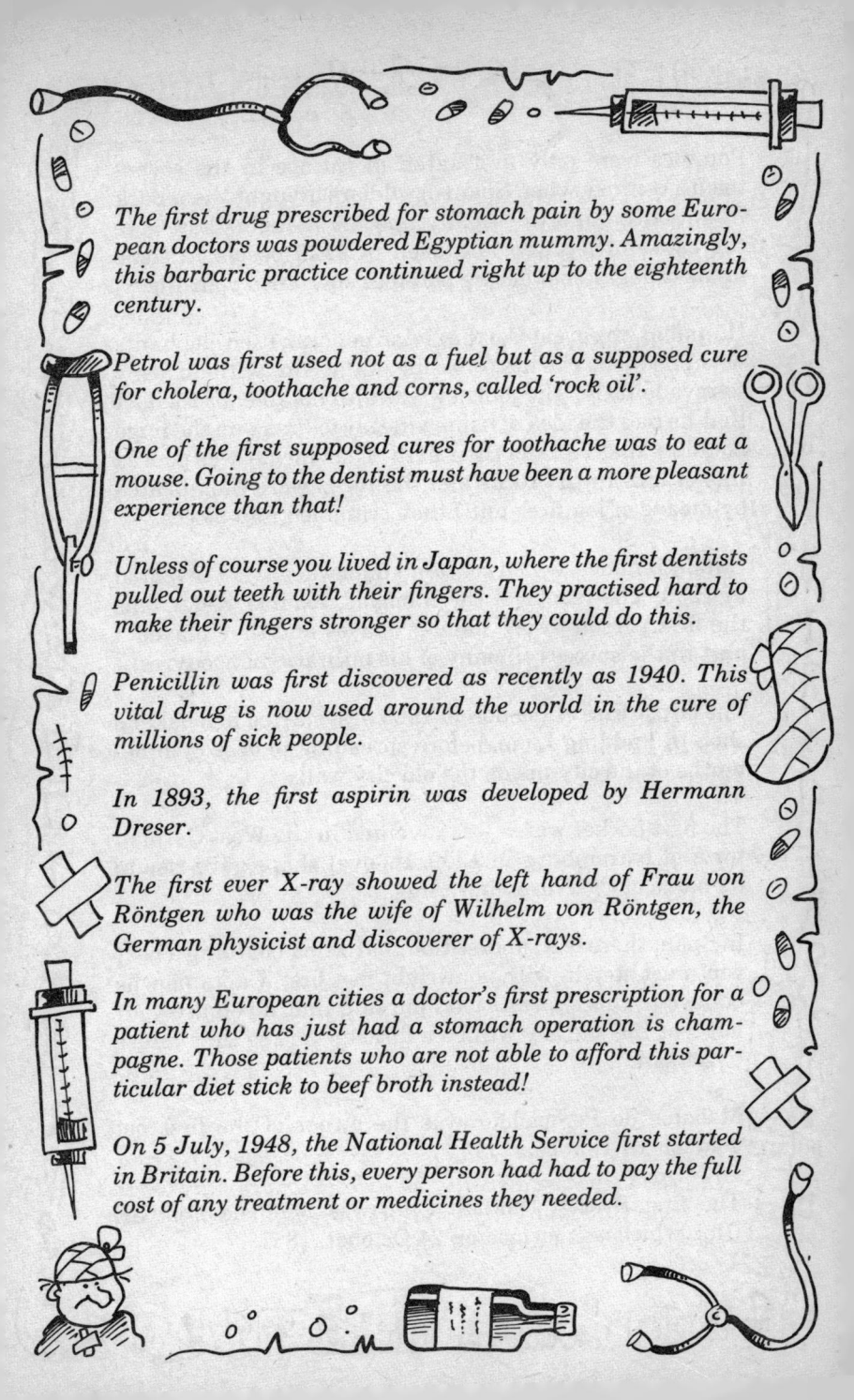

The first drug prescribed for stomach pain by some European doctors was powdered Egyptian mummy. Amazingly, this barbaric practice continued right up to the eighteenth century.

Petrol was first used not as a fuel but as a supposed cure for cholera, toothache and corns, called 'rock oil'.

One of the first supposed cures for toothache was to eat a mouse. Going to the dentist must have been a more pleasant experience than that!

Unless of course you lived in Japan, where the first dentists pulled out teeth with their fingers. They practised hard to make their fingers stronger so that they could do this.

Penicillin was first discovered as recently as 1940. This vital drug is now used around the world in the cure of millions of sick people.

In 1893, the first aspirin was developed by Hermann Dreser.

The first ever X-ray showed the left hand of Frau von Röntgen who was the wife of Wilhelm von Röntgen, the German physicist and discoverer of X-rays.

In many European cities a doctor's first prescription for a patient who has just had a stomach operation is champagne. Those patients who are not able to afford this particular diet stick to beef broth instead!

On 5 July, 1948, the National Health Service first started in Britain. Before this, every person had had to pay the full cost of any treatment or medicines they needed.

Potatoes were only first eaten in Europe in the seventeenth century when Spanish soldiers brought them back from South America. At first, people thought they were the cause of leprosy, and even in 1720 people in some areas thought that eating potatoes shortened your life.

Hannibal, the great Carthaginian general, used elephants when he made the first crossing of the Alps with an army to invade Italy. The journey was also notable for the fact that he had the idea of using vinegar to break up the huge boulders that blocked their path. The vinegar was poured into cracks in the rocks and the rocks were then heated by means of log fires until they crumbled into pieces.

Hand-grenades, which contain gunpowder, were invented in 1230. The leader of the Mongols, Khubla Khan, was the first person to use hand-grenades and they played a part in the success of many of his military manoeuvres.

The Great Fire of London in 1666 first started in a baker's shop in Pudding Lane, before spreading to destroy nine-tenths of the city inside the old city walls.

The first pocket watch was invented in the West German town of Nuremburg in 1509. Its oval shape gave rise to its name of the Nuremburg Egg.

In Spain there is a superstition that when boarding a boat you must step in with your right foot first. Captains who believe in this superstition maintain that if you use your left foot the journey will be a disaster and so they refuse to set sail.

Madame de Pompadour was the owner of the first pet goldfish in France.

The first British Football Club was Sheffield Football Club which was formed on 24 October, 1857.

In Florida, restaurants serve rattlesnake as a first-course delicacy.

Ether was the first anaesthetic to be used for operations. Its use was discovered entirely by chance when a chemistry student saw the effect it had on friends who were breathing it at parties. The original attempts to use it as an anaesthetic were met with accusations of sorcery and threats of death. Surgery has come a long way since then and, nowadays, doctors would not think of performing an operation without an anaesthetic.

China was the first country to use paper in AD 107.

The first time that a Christian navy was successful in battle against a Moslem one was also the last time that a sea battle was fought using boats powered by oars. It took place at Lepanto in Greece in 1571.

The first known pictures of bows are in Mesolithic cave paintings in Spain. Archery appears not to have developed as an organised sport until the third century AD, although there is some evidence to suggest that competitive archery may have originated in the twelfth century.

When the now famous annual cricket match between the schools of Eton and Harrow was first played in 1805, the great poet Lord Byron was in the Harrow team.

The most popular first name in the world is Mohammed.

The first Englishman to be given two Christian names when he was baptised was Henry Frederick, the Earl of Arundel, who died in 1680.

The first special effects in modern theatres were often created by the use of pollen. Pollen is a highly flammable substance and it could be used to create stage lighting by throwing pollen grains on to a red hot shovel.

There is an old custom in the countryside that a sprig of mistletoe is given to the first cow in a herd to have a calf at the start of the New Year. This is said to protect the herd from bad luck in the coming year.

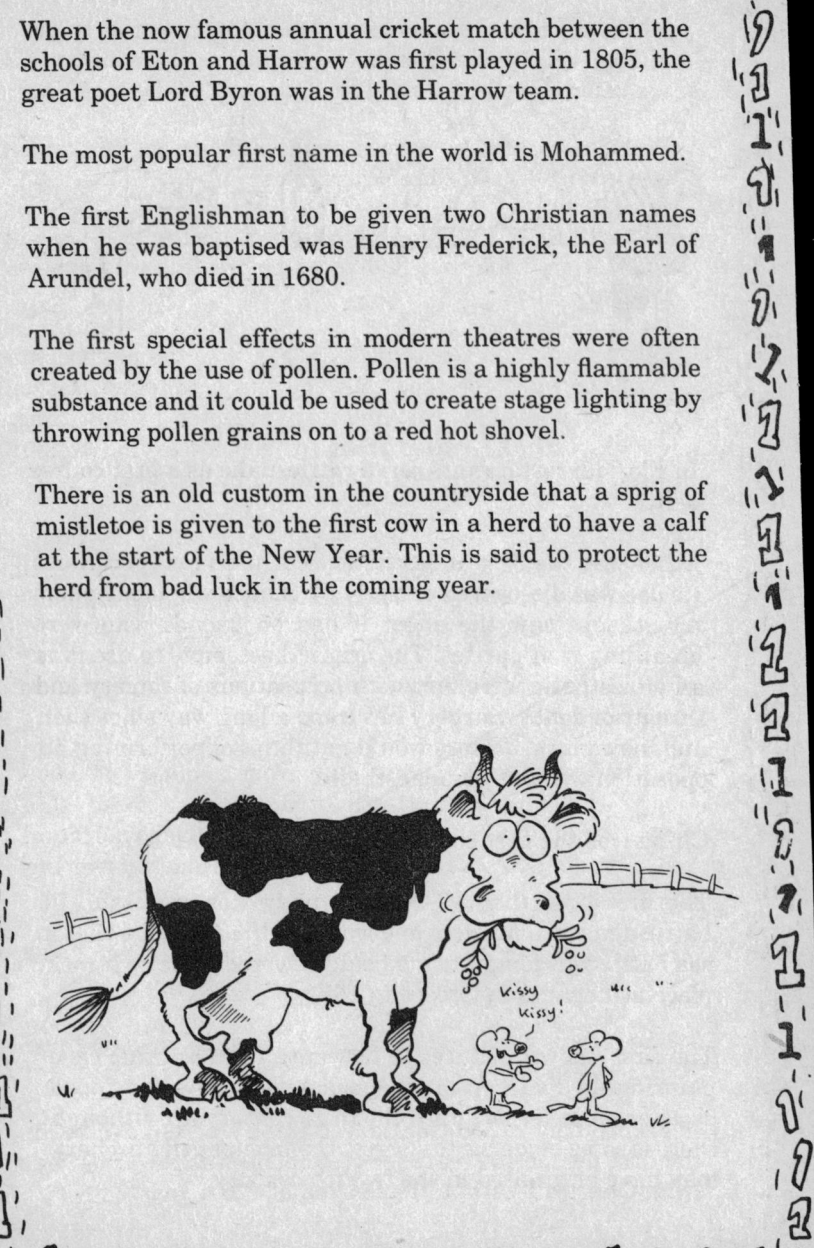

Playing cards first became popular during the reign of Henry VII, so the Queen's face shown on the cards in a traditional pack is that of his Queen, Elizabeth of York.

When beer first became a popular drink in England it was often served at breakfast time.

Houses in Paris were given numbers for the first time in 1463. It took another 300 years before this was done in London.

Anaxagoras, the Greek philosopher, was the first person to put forward the idea that the sun was round, rather than a flat disc as was generally accepted at that time. He was actually exiled from Athens for saying that it might be a rock glowing hundreds of miles away.

Battersea Dogs' Home, first opened as a refuge for homeless dogs in 1871, cares for more than 20,000 dogs each year. Sadly, many of these have to be put down if homes cannot be found for them.

Oil in the North Sea was first struck by British Petroleum on 1 September, 1965.

The first flowering plants date from about 65,000,000 years ago. This is the estimated age of a fossil of a flowering plant with palm-like imprints which was found in Colorado, USA in 1953 and which is the oldest flowering plant fossil to have been found.

The first proper fire brigade was formed almost 2,000 years ago by the Emperor Augustus in Rome.

When X-rays were first discovered, Lord Kelvin said they 'will prove to be a hoax'.

A French chef called Gerald Tissain is said to have been the first person to create ice-cream. He was rewarded by King Charles I with a life pension of £20 a year.

The first American satellite launched at Cape Canaveral, USA, in 1957 exploded before it had risen more than one metre off the ground.

The pendulum clock was first developed in the seventeenth century and was the first clock to keep time completely accurately.

In times gone by, salt was the most valuable commodity known. Its importance to man was so great that explorers were sent around the world in search of it. As a result people were sometimes paid in salt rather than money and this gave rise to the word 'salary' which means payment.

The nineteenth-century Scottish missionary and explorer, David Livingstone, was the first European to discover the Victoria Falls in Africa.

The first Christmas cards were produced in 1843.

In 1698 the first Eddystone lighthouse was built on Eddystone Rocks in the English Channel, south-west of Plymouth. It was made entirely of wood and survived for four years before being destroyed by a storm.

The first controlled flight in a powered aircraft was made by the American, Orville Wright, in 1903. The length of the flight was actually shorter than the length of a jumbo jet and lasted only twelve seconds. The announcement of this event did not make much impression on the world's news reporters and in Britain, only one newspaper made a mention of it.

The phrase to 'lick into shape' was first coined in connection with new-born bear cubs. People used to think that they were born as shapeless masses of flesh which had to be literally licked into shape by their mother!

FASHIONABLE FIRSTS

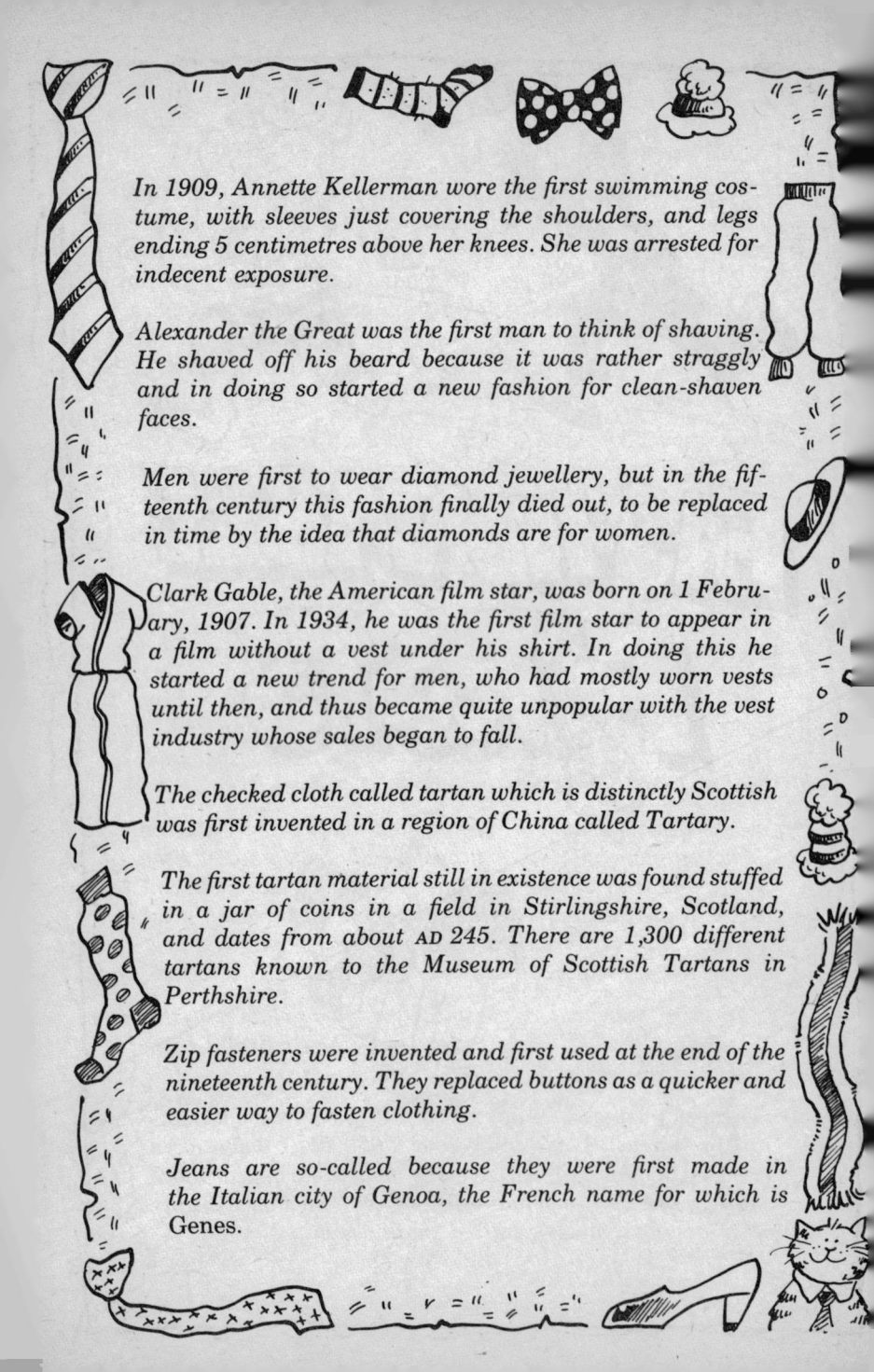

In 1909, Annette Kellerman wore the first swimming costume, with sleeves just covering the shoulders, and legs ending 5 centimetres above her knees. She was arrested for indecent exposure.

Alexander the Great was the first man to think of shaving. He shaved off his beard because it was rather straggly and in doing so started a new fashion for clean-shaven faces.

Men were first to wear diamond jewellery, but in the fifteenth century this fashion finally died out, to be replaced in time by the idea that diamonds are for women.

Clark Gable, the American film star, was born on 1 February, 1907. In 1934, he was the first film star to appear in a film without a vest under his shirt. In doing this he started a new trend for men, who had mostly worn vests until then, and thus became quite unpopular with the vest industry whose sales began to fall.

The checked cloth called tartan which is distinctly Scottish was first invented in a region of China called Tartary.

The first tartan material still in existence was found stuffed in a jar of coins in a field in Stirlingshire, Scotland, and dates from about AD 245. There are 1,300 different tartans known to the Museum of Scottish Tartans in Perthshire.

Zip fasteners were invented and first used at the end of the nineteenth century. They replaced buttons as a quicker and easier way to fasten clothing.

Jeans are so-called because they were first made in the Italian city of Genoa, the French name for which is Genes.

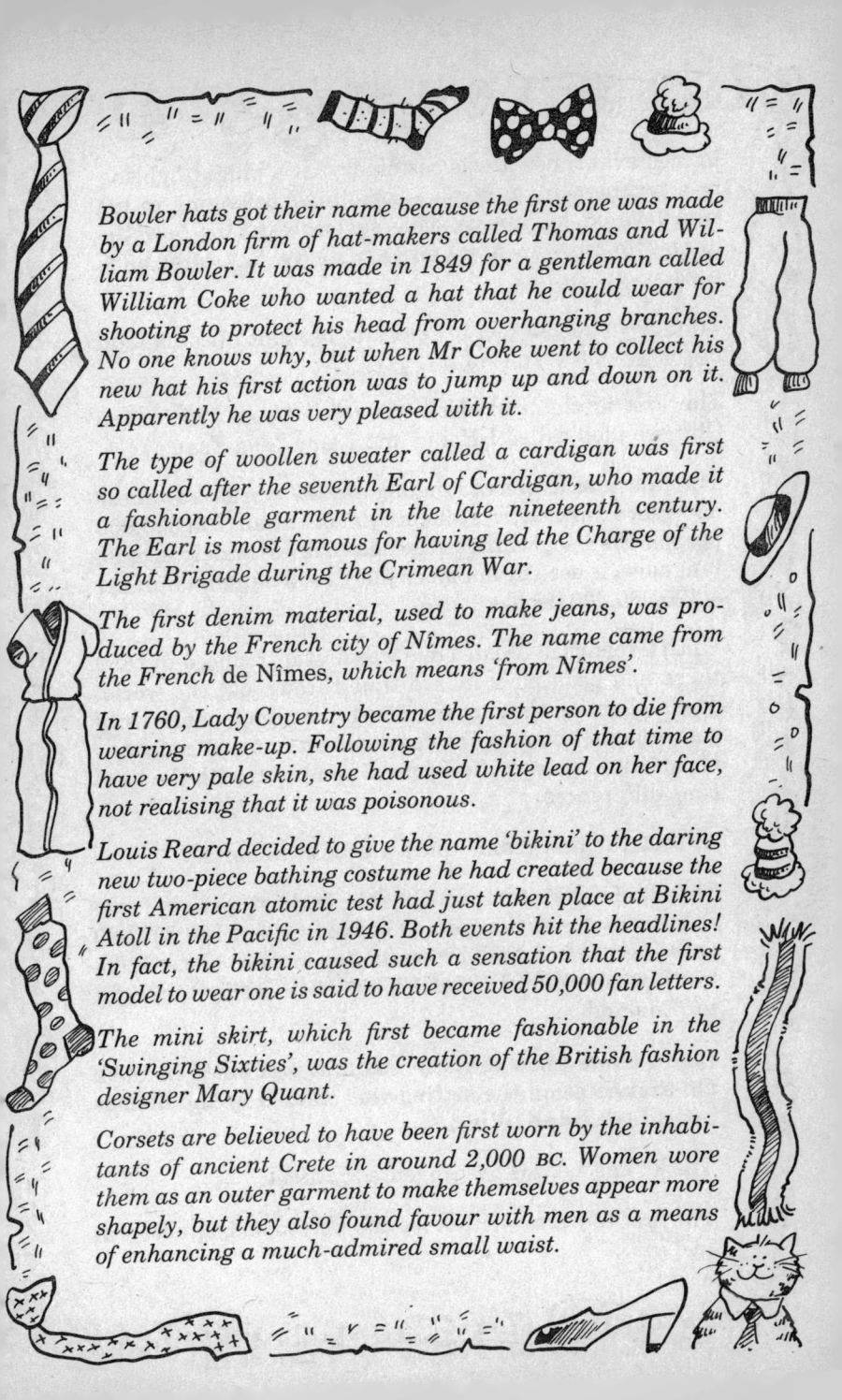

Bowler hats got their name because the first one was made by a London firm of hat-makers called Thomas and William Bowler. It was made in 1849 for a gentleman called William Coke who wanted a hat that he could wear for shooting to protect his head from overhanging branches. No one knows why, but when Mr Coke went to collect his new hat his first action was to jump up and down on it. Apparently he was very pleased with it.

The type of woollen sweater called a cardigan was first so called after the seventh Earl of Cardigan, who made it a fashionable garment in the late nineteenth century. The Earl is most famous for having led the Charge of the Light Brigade during the Crimean War.

The first denim material, used to make jeans, was produced by the French city of Nîmes. The name came from the French de Nîmes, which means 'from Nîmes'.

In 1760, Lady Coventry became the first person to die from wearing make-up. Following the fashion of that time to have very pale skin, she had used white lead on her face, not realising that it was poisonous.

Louis Reard decided to give the name 'bikini' to the daring new two-piece bathing costume he had created because the first American atomic test had just taken place at Bikini Atoll in the Pacific in 1946. Both events hit the headlines! In fact, the bikini caused such a sensation that the first model to wear one is said to have received 50,000 fan letters.

The mini skirt, which first became fashionable in the 'Swinging Sixties', was the creation of the British fashion designer Mary Quant.

Corsets are believed to have been first worn by the inhabitants of ancient Crete in around 2,000 BC. Women wore them as an outer garment to make themselves appear more shapely, but they also found favour with men as a means of enhancing a much-admired small waist.

In medieval times it was customary for a knight fighting in a tournament to display something belonging to his true love on his sleeve. This custom explains how the phrase 'to pin your heart on your sleeve' first came to be used.

Thimbles made of metal were first brought into England in the seventeenth century.

The first mechanical clock was made in AD 725 by two Chinese men called I-Hsing and Liang Ling-Tsan.

The first and foremost language in the world is Chinese or 'Guoyo', which is spoken by more than 700,000,000 people. English, which is the second most widely spoken language, is used by not much more than half that number – 395,000,000 people.

Until Greenwich Mean Time was first introduced in 1880 there had been no standard time throughout the world. The realisation that an organised system was a necessity was brought about by the development in many countries of railways, which suffered great confusion with the local time differences.

In 1496 the first tennis court was built in Paris.

The Maiden-hair tree, which is the earliest species of tree still surviving, first appeared in China about 160,000,000 years ago. It has been grown in Japan since about 1100, but it was not until about 1754 that it was first brought to England.

Ballet as we know it today was first performed in 1489. On that occasion the setting was created by the famous artist Leonardo da Vinci.

The jet engine was first invented in 1944.

The first concerto written for and played on bagpipes was in 1755.

It was Aristotle, the Greek philosopher, who first recorded the old saying 'One swallow does not make a summer'.

The caves of Nerja near Malaga in Spain were first discovered by accident in 1959 by four boys playing in the area. They are now famous for their enormous display of weirdly formed stalactites and stalagmites, which include the world's longest known stalactite, measuring 59 metres and extending from the roof right to the floor.

Mr and Mrs Ralph Cummins had five children, the first of whom was born on 20 February, 1952. Extraordinarily, each of the other four was also born on that day in successive years. The 20th of February must have been a rather expensive day for them with so many birthdays to celebrate!

When babies are first born they have about 350 bones in their bodies. Some of these gradually fuse together during the growing process, so that adults only have 206 bones.

The planet Pluto, which is the smallest of the nine major planets in the solar system and the furthest from the sun, was first discovered in 1930. It takes 248 years to complete its orbit of the sun.

The first nylon stockings were made in 1937.

Protista, the simplest known living organisms consisting of a single cell and only visible when viewed under a microscope, were first discovered in 1676 by a Dutch biologist.

The Society of Friends, known as Quakers, was first so called because George Fox, its founder, told people that they should 'quake and tremble at the word of the Lord'.

The term 'a white elephant', which refers to an unwanted gift, was first used as a result of the actions of a certain King of Siam. He hit upon the plan of giving a rare white elephant to people who displeased him and became his enemies. The 'gift' so burdened them, because the elephant was very expensive to feed and they did not dare to destroy so valuable an animal, that they went bankrupt!

The five continents of the world all have names in which the first letter is the same as the last one. In four of them that letter is A – America, Australia, Asia and Antarctica. The fifth one, and the odd one out with an E, is Europe.

When the word 'Queen' first became part of the English language its meaning was quite different from that used today. It developed from two sources, the Old English *cwen* meaning simply 'woman' and the word *quean* meaning 'worthless woman'. Not at all the same as our royal title!

The first wheeled vehicle to be landed on the Moon was Lunakhod 1 on 17 November, 1970. It was controlled from Earth and travelled a total of 10.54 kilometres.

The first recorded earthquake in Britain was in AD 974.

When oil was first used in the 1850s the petrol that was produced as a by-product was not used for anything.

Harrods, the famous London department store, was the first place in England to install an escalator in 1898. It was such a novelty that many shoppers were overcome with excitement and the store had to position men at the top to administer reviving doses of brandy or smelling salts!

In November 1989 Mr Albert Wood became Britain's oldest first-time home buyer at the age of 93, when he completed arrangements for a mortgage to buy a council flat in West Sussex.

The 'monkey' wrench or spanner has nothing to do with monkeys! The name was first spelt 'moncke' because its inventor was Charles Moncke, but over the years it has become transformed.

The 'Iron Curtain' has been much used as a descriptive term distinguishing between the Communist countries and the West. It was first used in a speech by Winston Churchill in Fulton, Missouri, USA, in 1946 when he said 'An iron curtain has descended upon Europe.'

The idea of using gas as a means of lighting was first thought of in England in 1787.

Nelson's Column was first built in London's Trafalgar Square in 1840 at a cost of £46,000.

In 1900 the loudspeaker was first used on top of the Eiffel Tower in Paris.

The idea for sailors to have a daily tot of rum mixed with water was first introduced in 1731 by Admiral Edward Vernon, who believed that watered rum, or 'grog' as it was known, slightly reduced sickness among sailors. The daily ration was abolished in 1970.

Barbados was first so called because Portuguese sailors who landed there in the sixteenth century found bearded fig trees growing on the island which led them to name it *Los barbados* – 'the bearded ones'.

The title of the Emperor of Rome, 'Caesar', was the first of a number of different words that originated from the same source. Others were the German word *Kaiser*, meaning Emperor, and the Russian word *Czar*.

In medieval times people believed that the leopard was a cross between a lion and a white panther, and so they based its name on the Greek word *leo* for lion and *pard* which was their name for the white panther.

The red flag with the hammer and sickle symbols of the USSR was first used in 1917.

GETTING THERE FARSTS

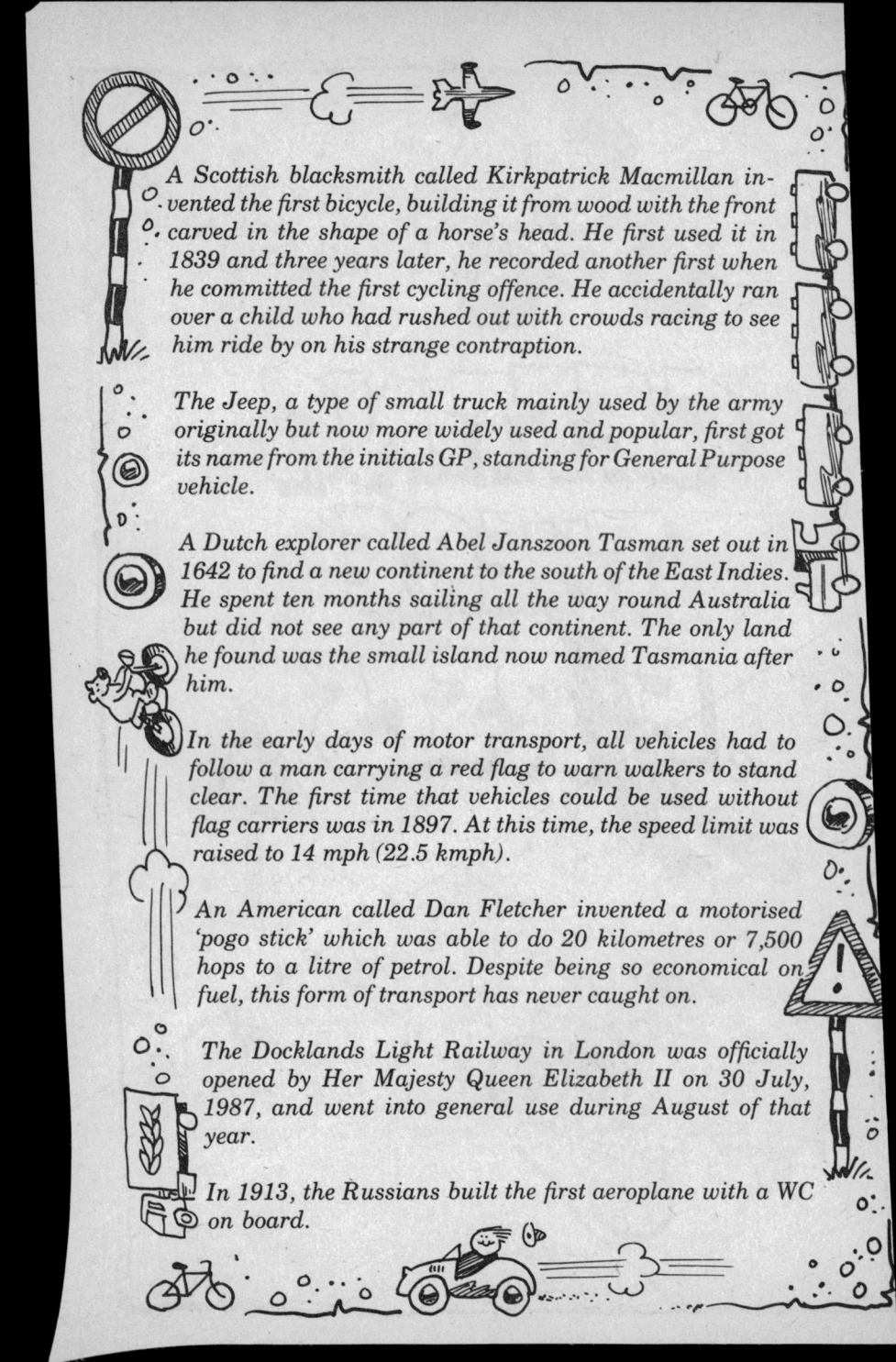

A Scottish blacksmith called Kirkpatrick Macmillan invented the first bicycle, building it from wood with the front carved in the shape of a horse's head. He first used it in 1839 and three years later, he recorded another first when he committed the first cycling offence. He accidentally ran over a child who had rushed out with crowds racing to see him ride by on his strange contraption.

The Jeep, a type of small truck mainly used by the army originally but now more widely used and popular, first got its name from the initials GP, standing for General Purpose vehicle.

A Dutch explorer called Abel Janszoon Tasman set out in 1642 to find a new continent to the south of the East Indies. He spent ten months sailing all the way round Australia but did not see any part of that continent. The only land he found was the small island now named Tasmania after him.

In the early days of motor transport, all vehicles had to follow a man carrying a red flag to warn walkers to stand clear. The first time that vehicles could be used without flag carriers was in 1897. At this time, the speed limit was raised to 14 mph (22.5 kmph).

An American called Dan Fletcher invented a motorised 'pogo stick' which was able to do 20 kilometres or 7,500 hops to a litre of petrol. Despite being so economical on fuel, this form of transport has never caught on.

The Docklands Light Railway in London was officially opened by Her Majesty Queen Elizabeth II on 30 July, 1987, and went into general use during August of that year.

In 1913, the Russians built the first aeroplane with a WC on board.

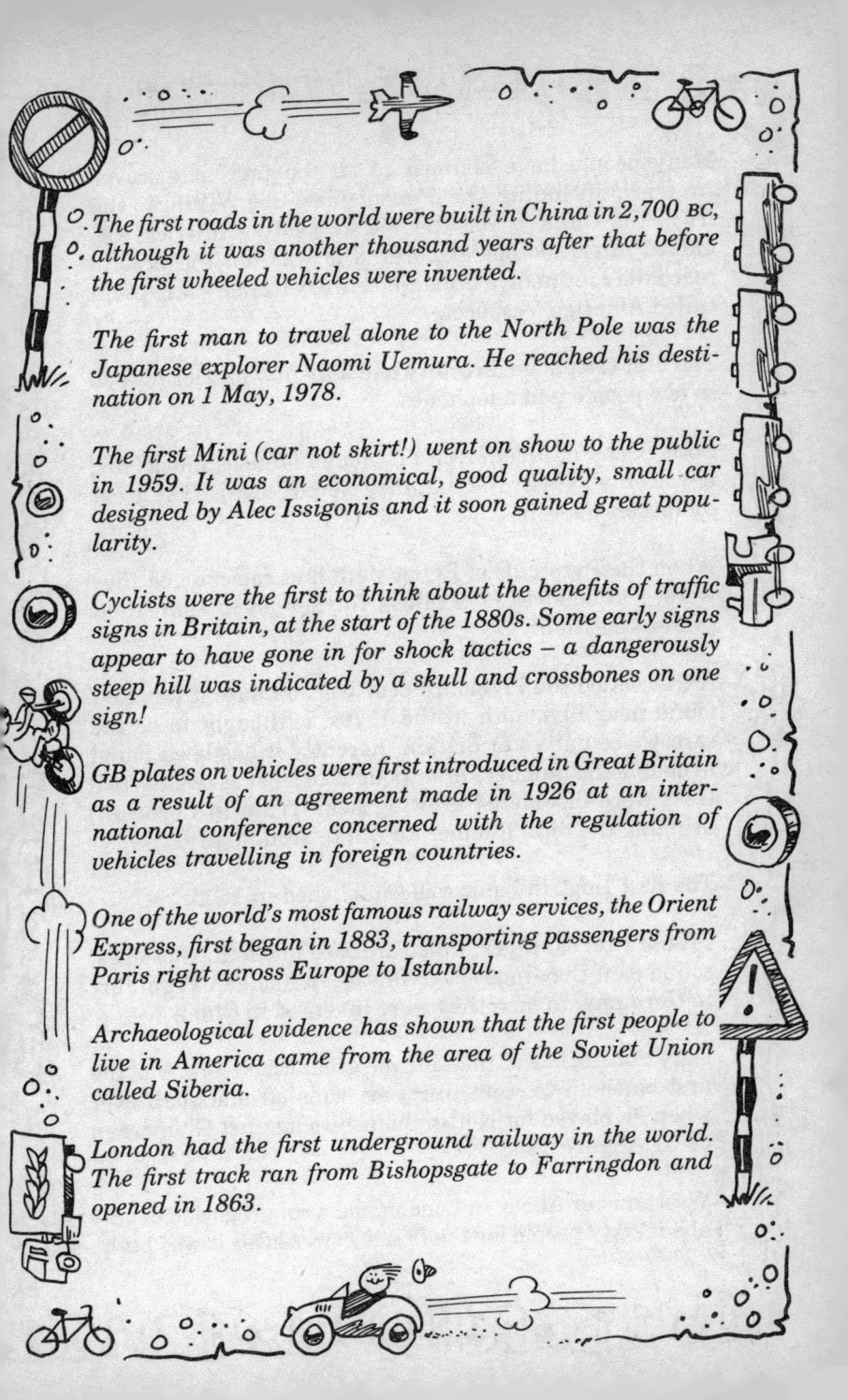

The first roads in the world were built in China in 2,700 BC, although it was another thousand years after that before the first wheeled vehicles were invented.

The first man to travel alone to the North Pole was the Japanese explorer Naomi Uemura. He reached his destination on 1 May, 1978.

The first Mini (car not skirt!) went on show to the public in 1959. It was an economical, good quality, small car designed by Alec Issigonis and it soon gained great popularity.

Cyclists were the first to think about the benefits of traffic signs in Britain, at the start of the 1880s. Some early signs appear to have gone in for shock tactics – a dangerously steep hill was indicated by a skull and crossbones on one sign!

GB plates on vehicles were first introduced in Great Britain as a result of an agreement made in 1926 at an international conference concerned with the regulation of vehicles travelling in foreign countries.

One of the world's most famous railway services, the Orient Express, first began in 1883, transporting passengers from Paris right across Europe to Istanbul.

Archaeological evidence has shown that the first people to live in America came from the area of the Soviet Union called Siberia.

London had the first underground railway in the world. The first track ran from Bishopsgate to Farringdon and opened in 1863.

Many people have claimed to be the first to discover America, including the Phoenicians, the Vikings, the Irish, the Chinese and the Welsh. Oddly, America was named after another explorer who was not the first to reach the continent, a fifteenth-century Italian sea captain called Amerigo Vespucci.

The first telephone directory had only fifty entries in it as so few people had telephones.

Both Bach and Beethoven first found fame as musicians; it was only in later life that they were recognised as great composers as well.

When the Pyramids of Egypt were first constructed they were 4 kilometres (2½ miles) further north than their present position.

A tree called the Plymouth pear tree, because it was first found near Plymouth in the 1870s, is thought to be the rarest tree native to Britain. Recently it has been found in double the numbers first thought to exist as twenty-two trees were discovered growing near Truro in Cornwall, bringing the total number known to around fifty.

The first English bank was established in 1603.

Frankfurter sausages, which are used in making hot-dogs, sound as if they must have first been made in Frankfurt in Germany. In fact, they were invented in China.

Gary Sobers, one of the all-time great cricketers, was the first batsman to score thirty-six runs off a six-ball over when he played for Nottinghamshire against Glamorgan on 31 August, 1968.

Westminster Abbey in London had a congregation of only about sixty people for the first services after it was built.

The disastrous sinking of the SS *Titanic* with its massive loss of life was seemingly uncannily first predicted in 1898, fourteen years before it happened, in a novel by the writer Morgan Robertson. In his book, Robertson featured a liner the same size as the *Titanic*, which could carry the same number of passengers but which, like the *Titanic*, did not provide enough safety equipment for that number. The story told how the ship hit an iceberg in the North Atlantic and sank in more or less the same area as the *Titanic* did in real life, not long after in 1912. Most weird of all must certainly be the fact that Robertson called the ship in his story the *Titan*.

The first cheque was printed in 1760.

Dr Alexander Fleming is well known as the discoverer of penicillin, one of the most important and widely used drugs in medicine, which he first found in mould. Less well known is the fact that the Aborigines were using mould from trees to help heal their wounds long before Dr Fleming's discovery.

The first and only President of the Confederate States of America was Jefferson Davis from 1861 to 1865.

When the word 'silly' was first used it meant holy, coming from the German word *selig*. Gradually, however, its meaning has changed and instead of being used to describe innocent people, it is now used to mean foolishly gullible people.

In 1989 the Post Office issued a new kind of Christmas stamp. For the first time, stamps went on sale with a 1p premium to raise money for charity.

John Walker, who first invented matches, felt that he ought not to keep the exclusive right to such an important invention, so he did not patent his discovery and as a result made no money from it.

The building of a tunnel under the English Channel to link Britain by rail with the rest of Europe is currently in progress, but the idea of a tunnel was first suggested in Napoleon's reign. It was rejected by the British eighty years later in 1880 on the basis that it would make Britain easier to attack.

In general, the first foot that a person puts into their trousers when getting dressed indicates whether they are left- or right-handed.

There is a proverb which says 'On the first of March, the crows begin to search'. This refers to the fact that one of the first signs of spring is the pairing of birds, and the crow is among the first to search for and find a mate every year.

The equals sign (=) was used for the first time in an algebra text book printed in 1557.

The Moors who conquered Spain in the seventh century first originated from what was then called Mauritania but is today the part of Africa occupied by Algeria and Morocco. Mauritania itself now lies further to the west.

The Punch and Judy public house in London's Covent Garden is so-called to commemorate the first performance of Mr Punch's puppet show which took place within the rails of the Market as witnessed by Samuel Pepys in 1662.

Volleyball was invented in the USA in 1895 for older men and women to play instead of basketball, which was considered too vigorous. How things change! The original gentle sport has now become a very fast and skilled game for fit people.

The first edition of the gospels written in the language spoken by Eskimos was published in 1744.

In November 1989, Craig Shergold, a nine-year-old boy suffering from cancer, became the first person to receive more than a million get-well cards. A nationwide appeal helped to achieve this and so fulfil his ambition to get an entry in the *Guinness Book of Records*.

Instant coffee may sound as if it is a recent invention, a forerunner of the 'fast food' approach to eating, but it was actually first drunk in 1838.

Nicaragua's Post Office issued a stamp to mark the first soccer World Cup in 1930, but they got the result wrong! The stamp was printed as Uruguay 4, Argentina 1, but the final score was 4–2 to Uruguay.

Scientists working in the Welsh town of Bangor invented a 'bleeper' to hang around the necks of sheep, making it possible for shepherds to find their sheep without leaving their homes. The bleeper was called 'Bangor Orange Position Estimating Equipment for Pastures', which shortens to the initials BO PEEP!

Geologists who have studied the rock formation in northern Scotland have suggested that this part of Great Britain may first have been an island hundreds of millions of years ago and then have become joined to the mainland by movements in the earth's crust.

The first alarm clock was made a long time ago, in 1350, by German monks who needed to wake up in time for early prayer meetings.

In Ancient Greece, a woman's age was counted as being from the first day of her married life.

Lawn tennis balls were at first made of plain rubber until, one day, a champion Real Tennis player called J. M. Heathcote found he couldn't control the balls on wet grass and asked his wife to make cloth covers for them. This was the start of modern tennis balls, which are made of cloth-covered rubber.

During the sixteenth century the first thing that people did if there was an outbreak of the plague in the area where they lived was to kiss a billy goat. They believed this protected them from the much-feared illness!

The first snow ever recorded in the middle of the Sahara desert fell in 1979.

Thomas Adams was trying to find a way to use a gumlike substance called chicle, which he thought might be a good substitute for rubber in industry. As he deliberated one day, he started to chew on a piece of chicle and this gave him the idea of adding flavouring to it and selling it as chewing-gum.

The month of January was first called after the Roman god Janus, who was the god of doorways with two faces for looking in either direction. He was believed to guard the 'doorway to the new year', that is the first month of the new year, or as we know it, January.

INVENTIVE FIRSTS

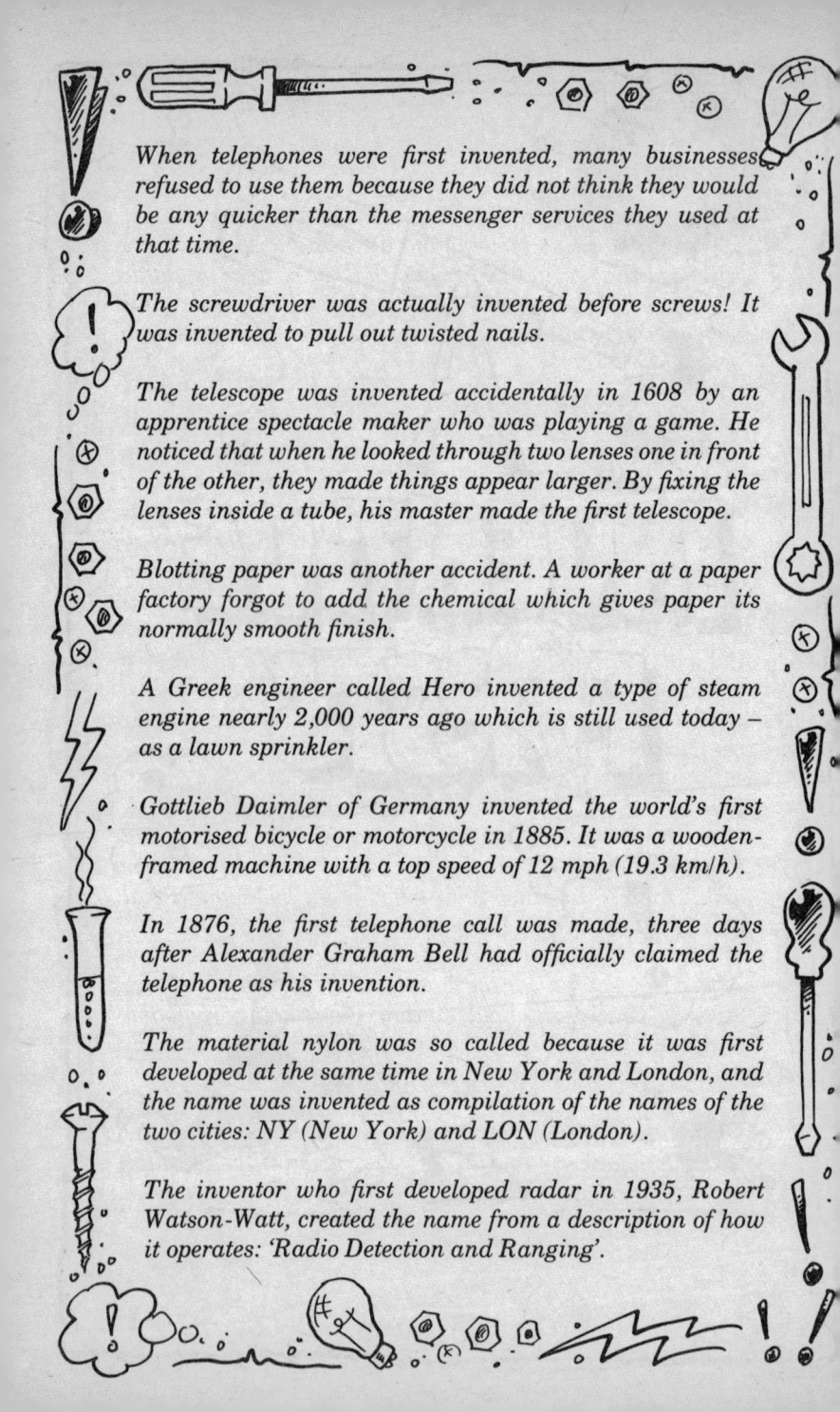

When telephones were first invented, many businesses refused to use them because they did not think they would be any quicker than the messenger services they used at that time.

The screwdriver was actually invented before screws! It was invented to pull out twisted nails.

The telescope was invented accidentally in 1608 by an apprentice spectacle maker who was playing a game. He noticed that when he looked through two lenses one in front of the other, they made things appear larger. By fixing the lenses inside a tube, his master made the first telescope.

Blotting paper was another accident. A worker at a paper factory forgot to add the chemical which gives paper its normally smooth finish.

A Greek engineer called Hero invented a type of steam engine nearly 2,000 years ago which is still used today – as a lawn sprinkler.

Gottlieb Daimler of Germany invented the world's first motorised bicycle or motorcycle in 1885. It was a wooden-framed machine with a top speed of 12 mph (19.3 km/h).

In 1876, the first telephone call was made, three days after Alexander Graham Bell had officially claimed the telephone as his invention.

The material nylon was so called because it was first developed at the same time in New York and London, and the name was invented as compilation of the names of the two cities: NY (New York) and LON (London).

The inventor who first developed radar in 1935, Robert Watson-Watt, created the name from a description of how it operates: 'Radio Detection and Ranging'.

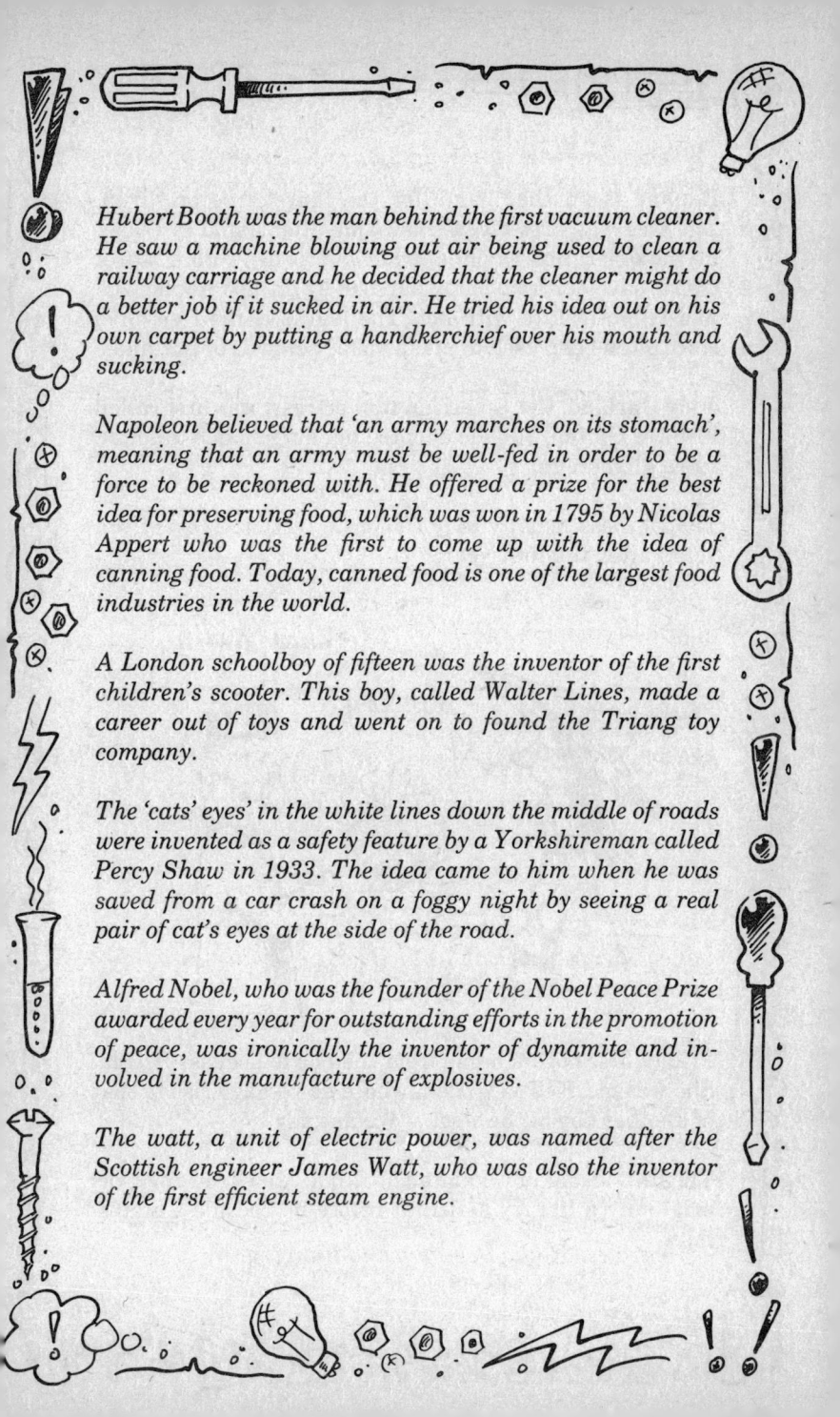

Hubert Booth was the man behind the first vacuum cleaner. He saw a machine blowing out air being used to clean a railway carriage and he decided that the cleaner might do a better job if it sucked in air. He tried his idea out on his own carpet by putting a handkerchief over his mouth and sucking.

Napoleon believed that 'an army marches on its stomach', meaning that an army must be well-fed in order to be a force to be reckoned with. He offered a prize for the best idea for preserving food, which was won in 1795 by Nicolas Appert who was the first to come up with the idea of canning food. Today, canned food is one of the largest food industries in the world.

A London schoolboy of fifteen was the inventor of the first children's scooter. This boy, called Walter Lines, made a career out of toys and went on to found the Triang toy company.

The 'cats' eyes' in the white lines down the middle of roads were invented as a safety feature by a Yorkshireman called Percy Shaw in 1933. The idea came to him when he was saved from a car crash on a foggy night by seeing a real pair of cat's eyes at the side of the road.

Alfred Nobel, who was the founder of the Nobel Peace Prize awarded every year for outstanding efforts in the promotion of peace, was ironically the inventor of dynamite and involved in the manufacture of explosives.

The watt, a unit of electric power, was named after the Scottish engineer James Watt, who was also the inventor of the first efficient steam engine.

Daphne is another name for the laurel tree or shrub. The tree was first given this name after a girl in Greek mythology called Daphne, who was turned into a laurel tree to save her from being pursued by the god Apollo who had fallen in love with her. The leaves of the tree have since often been used to make victory crowns or garlands.

Judy Garland, the American film actress, was first called Frances Gumm, but she adopted her stage name to sound more glamorous.

The Chinese usually only celebrate birthdays every ten years after the first year.

Friday first got its name from the Norse goddess Frigga. She was married to Woden, whose name gave rise to that of another day of the week – Wednesday.

The first leader of Communist China, Mao Tse-tung, was originally a library assistant before he became a statesman.

The first thing done by many so-called 'gauchos', or South American cowboys, before they set out for a day's riding is to put a piece of raw steak under their saddle. This way they finish up with a nice tender piece of meat to cook for supper as a result of the constant bumping up and down through the day.

Tristao da Cunha was the first person to set foot on the island in the South Atlantic which is called Tristan da Cunha after him. It is the remotest *inhabited* island in the world. The first person to live there permanently was Thomas Currie, who landed on the island in 1810.

Benedict IX was only 12 years old when he was first made Pope.

Tarmacadam, or 'tarmac' as it is usually called, was the invention of John MacAdam. He was the first person to have the idea of using small stones to make roads rather than large bumpy cobbles, and by using the tarmac he had invented he was able to build roads that stayed smooth and solid when ordinary roads were broken up by frost.

The first windscreen wipers were fitted on cars in Britain in 1921, but they had to be operated by hand!

The world's largest zoological reserve, the Etosha National Park in Namibia, was first established as long ago as 1907. It has gradually grown to its present size of 99,525 square kilometres.

Playing cards are thought to have first been used by the Chinese in 1120. In the fifteenth century in England, an Act of Parliament was passed to stop any more foreign cards from being imported as the game had become so popular.

There are now fifty states in the United States of America, compared with thirteen when it was first formed.

The first printed book, which was produced in China in AD 848, was made by carving each page out of a block of wood.

The feast of St Oswald was at first held on 29 February, but early this century complaints were made that because of leap years the festival could only be celebrated once every four years, so it was moved back a day to 28 February.

Spiro is the most popular first name on the Greek island of Corfu – more than fifty per cent of the island's men have this name.

Wellington boots are named after the Duke of Wellington, who won the battle of Waterloo against Napoleon in 1815. Although nowadays they are used to keep feet dry in rainy weather, Wellington first wore his boots for going into battle.

As is the case with so many useful inventions, dry cleaning was first discovered by mistake. Having accidentally spilt some spirit from a lamp on to a tablecloth, Mr Jolly-Bevin of Paris noticed how much cleaner the parts of the cloth looked that had been covered in spirit. On this basis he started a business using the spirit as a cleaner, and 'dry' cleaning (without the use of water) was born!

The first successful flight across the English Channel was in 1785 in a hot-air balloon. Unfortunately, the balloon had started to get dangerously low as it floated a few metres from the French coast, so the two men aboard took off all their clothes and threw them out in a desperate bid to make the balloon lighter and ensure their arrival on French soil.

The so-called penny post first began in England in May 1840 with the issue of the Penny Black stamp. This was the first time that prepayment of postage was used for the delivery of letters and every letter cost one penny.

William Pitt first became Prime Minister of Great Britain when he was only twenty-four years old.

The famous 'Gold Rush' in America started when gold was first discovered in California in January 1848. But news travelled more slowly in those days – it took almost six months for the East Coast, on the other side of America, to hear about the gold!

The nursery rhyme 'Ring a ring a roses' is known first from the fourteenth century. In those days it had a quite different use. Far from being sung by children, it was chanted by people in the belief that it gave them protection from the plague of the Black Death. The 'rose' was a red patch on the skin of someone with the plague and the 'pocket full of posies' were the herbs and flowers people carried to protect themselves.

The European Community (EC), often called the Common Market, was first formed in 1958 by and for the benefit of six European countries: Belgium, France, Italy, Luxembourg, the Netherlands and West Germany. It was the first real attempt to unite western Europe economically.

The game of lacrosse which is played in many girls' schools was first played in the fifteenth century by the American Indian tribe called the Iroquois.

The English word 'barbarian', meaning uncivilised or foreign, first came from the early Greeks who thought all foreign languages sounded like stutterings of 'bar-bar-bar-bar' and so called foreigners *barbaroi*.

The United Nations (UN) was first set up in 1945. Its main aim is to maintain international peace and promote worldwide cooperation, and it concerns itself with world problems such as poverty, disease, education and pollution. The UN headquarters are in New York City.

Scientists think that in the course of the Earth's development there were at first three large continents, which subsequently joined to form a single super-continent named Pangaea. Pangaea then eventually started to split up and the continents as we know them today gradually took shape.

The Romans were a people with many beliefs and superstitions. One of these was that a household would have bad luck if a visitor entered with his left foot first, so everyone automatically stepped into houses with their right foot first. So strong was the Romans' belief that bad luck was associated with the left side, that we have a legacy of it in the word 'sinister' meaning evil – *sinister* is Latin for 'left'.

The first Christmas trees, or Norway Spruce as they are properly called, grew in America 80 million years ago.

Sri Lanka is the world's third largest tea producer, but it was first important as a coffee producer until a disease killed off all the coffee bushes.

The abacus was the first form of calculator. Invented over 5,000 years ago in China, it is still used in the Far East today. Calculations are made by moving beads, each of which represents a unit of ten, hundred or whatever, along rows of wire.

A Swedish scientist, Wilhelm Scheele, was the first to find the chemical fluorine, which helps our teeth to be strong and healthy. He made his discovery in 1771.

ANIMAL FIRSTS

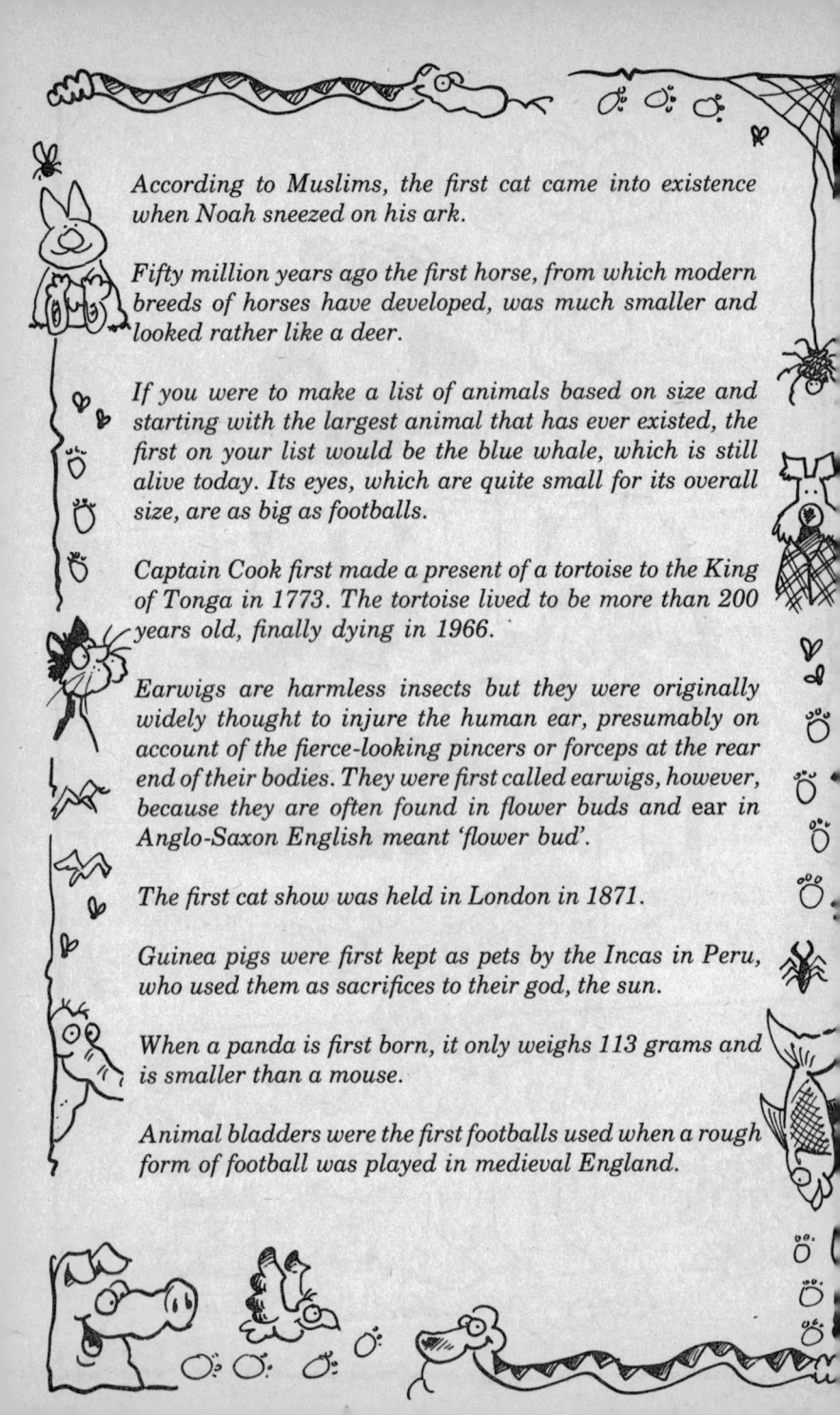

According to Muslims, the first cat came into existence when Noah sneezed on his ark.

Fifty million years ago the first horse, from which modern breeds of horses have developed, was much smaller and looked rather like a deer.

If you were to make a list of animals based on size and starting with the largest animal that has ever existed, the first on your list would be the blue whale, which is still alive today. Its eyes, which are quite small for its overall size, are as big as footballs.

Captain Cook first made a present of a tortoise to the King of Tonga in 1773. The tortoise lived to be more than 200 years old, finally dying in 1966.

Earwigs are harmless insects but they were originally widely thought to injure the human ear, presumably on account of the fierce-looking pincers or forceps at the rear end of their bodies. They were first called earwigs, however, because they are often found in flower buds and ear in Anglo-Saxon English meant 'flower bud'.

The first cat show was held in London in 1871.

Guinea pigs were first kept as pets by the Incas in Peru, who used them as sacrifices to their god, the sun.

When a panda is first born, it only weighs 113 grams and is smaller than a mouse.

Animal bladders were the first footballs used when a rough form of football was played in medieval England.

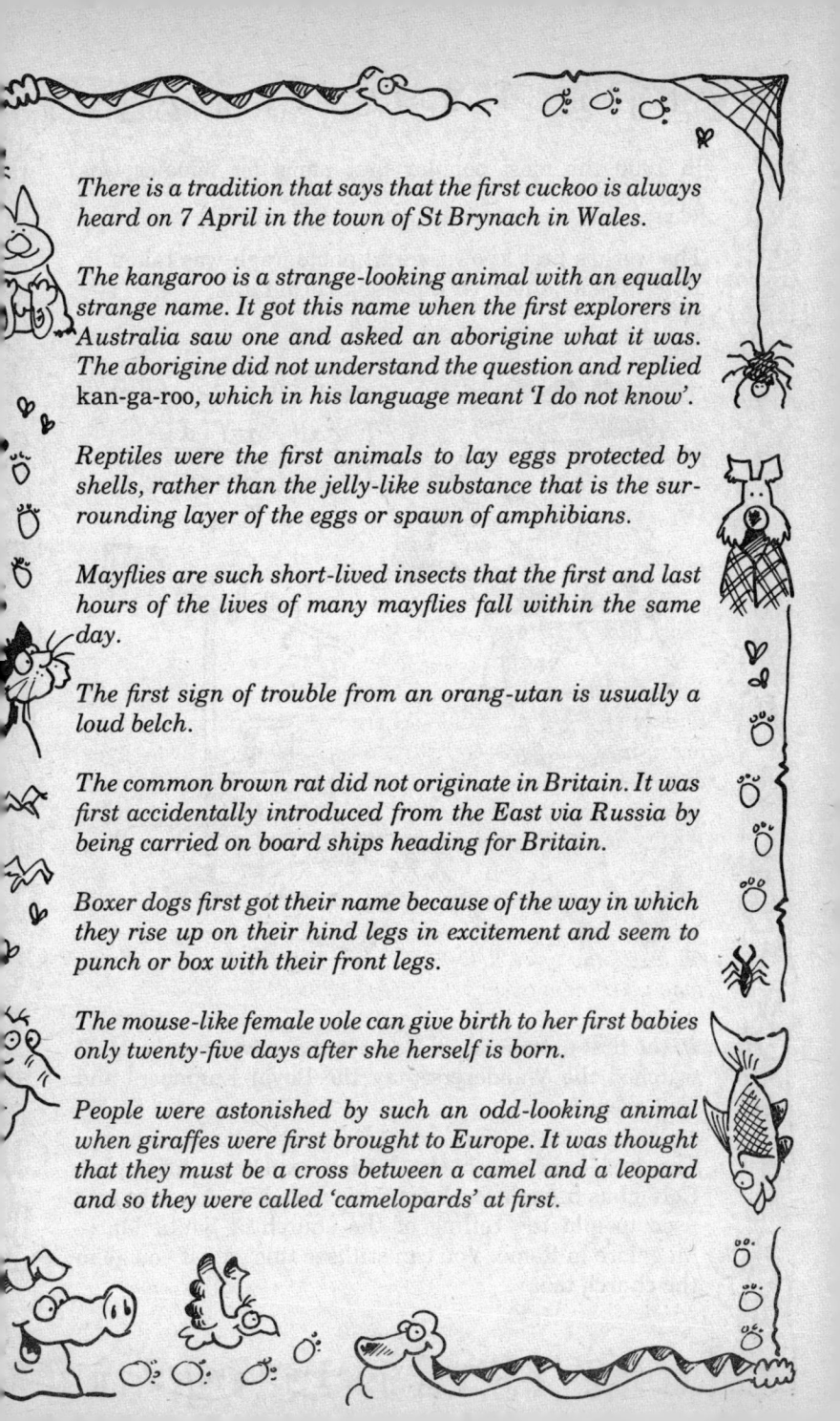

There is a tradition that says that the first cuckoo is always heard on 7 April in the town of St Brynach in Wales.

The kangaroo is a strange-looking animal with an equally strange name. It got this name when the first explorers in Australia saw one and asked an aborigine what it was. The aborigine did not understand the question and replied kan-ga-roo, which in his language meant 'I do not know'.

Reptiles were the first animals to lay eggs protected by shells, rather than the jelly-like substance that is the surrounding layer of the eggs or spawn of amphibians.

Mayflies are such short-lived insects that the first and last hours of the lives of many mayflies fall within the same day.

The first sign of trouble from an orang-utan is usually a loud belch.

The common brown rat did not originate in Britain. It was first accidentally introduced from the East via Russia by being carried on board ships heading for Britain.

Boxer dogs first got their name because of the way in which they rise up on their hind legs in excitement and seem to punch or box with their front legs.

The mouse-like female vole can give birth to her first babies only twenty-five days after she herself is born.

People were astonished by such an odd-looking animal when giraffes were first brought to Europe. It was thought that they must be a cross between a camel and a leopard and so they were called 'camelopards' at first.

In 1900 the most popular first name for females was Florence.

The world's first known aerial photograph was taken in 1858 from a balloon on the outskirts of Paris.

now this is what I call aerial photography!!

In the first ever Football Cup Final a crowd of only 2,000 watched the Wanderers play the Royal Engineers and beat them 1–0.

The first gold which the Italian explorer Christopher Columbus brought back from his voyage to America was used to gild the ceiling of the church of Santa Maria Maggiore in Rome. You can still see this gold if you go to the church today.

Number plates on cars were first introduced in France in 1893, but instead of a number as such, owners had to display their full name and address.

The Boy Scouts organisation was founded in 1908 by Sir Robert Baden-Powell. The first Boy Scout camp was attended by twenty boys.

The first and perhaps only experiment to find the depth of water that birds prefer to bathe in was conducted by the highly respected Audubon Society of America. They found that birds like a bath with 6 centimetres (2¼ inches) of water in it best.

The signs of the Zodiac were first so-called by the Greeks. The name refers to the animals.

Although it is now known that the tropical disease malaria is carried by mosquitoes, it was first believed to be caused by breathing what was thought of as stagnant, unhealthy air around bog land. This gave rise to its name which came from the Italian *mal aria* meaning 'bad air'.

In Korea everyone flies a kite during the first week of the New Year, and then lets it go to carry away bad luck.

Biscuits get their name from the French words *bis cuit* which means 'twice cooked' because at first biscuits were cooked twice to stop them from going stale.

Sir William Curtis was the first to use the phrase 'the three Rs' to describe the basic subjects first learnt by any child – reading, writing and arithmetic. The strange thing is that he himself could not read or write!

A palindrome is a word or phrase in which the first letter is the same as the last, the second is the same as the second from last, and so on, so that it reads the same backwards as forwards. 'Redivider' is the longest example of such a word in English.

The first sewing machine was developed by a Frenchman called Thimmonier in 1829.

'God bless you' may seem a strange thing to say when someone sneezes, but it was first used in ancient times because people believed that your soul left your body for a moment when you sneezed. Saying 'God bless you' was supposed to restore God's presence within you.

Surprisingly, Italy was not the first country to make spaghetti, macaroni, tortellini or any other kind of pasta. The great thirteenth-century explorer Marco Polo first saw pasta being made in China and decided to take the recipe back home to his native Italy.

The first city in the world to have a population in excess of one million was London.

The first car registration plate in Britain belonged to the Earl of Russell. It was simply 'A1'.

At the first attempt, Albert Einstein, who became a brilliant atomic scientist, failed to pass his entrance exams to university.

In 1989 opera-lovers in Britain were invited for the first time not only to hear and see an opera but also to smell it as well. For performances of Prokofiev's *The Love for Three Oranges* 'scratch 'n' sniff' cards offering six different, appropriate smells were placed on every seat. At a sign from the chorus, the audience used coins to scratch the appropriate panel releasing a smell to add to the atmosphere of the opera.

After a twenty-five-year campaign, proceedings inside the House of Commons were televised for the first ever time on Tuesday 21 November, 1989, when a new session of Parliament was opened by the Queen. Mr Ian Gow became the first MP to make a speech in front of the cameras, having been chosen by the Prime Minister to move the Loyal Address.

The first of the 'White Horse' hill carvings that still exist in Britain today is the Uffington White Horse in Oxfordshire, which dates from the late Iron Age (about 150 BC). It measures 114 metres (365 feet) from nose to tail and is 36 metres (115 feet) high.

Commercial television first went on the air in Britain on 22 September, 1955. The first advertisement shown was for Gibbs' SR toothpaste.

On 2 November, 1924, the *Sunday Express* newspaper carried the first ever crossword puzzle to appear in Britain.

In 1896 the first Modern Olympic Games was held in Athens, with only nine nations taking part.

The sense of smell is the first of the five senses that people tend to lose as they grow older.

Before he became a well-known film star Kirk Douglas was first called Issur Danielovitch Demsky.

Christmas is often written in the shortened form 'Xmas', which was first used in the Middle Ages because X was the first letter of Christ's name in Greek.

Compared with dinosaurs the first elephants were tiny, being only about the size of a pig. Present-day elephants average 5½ tonnes in weight, which is more than seventy times the weight of the average man.

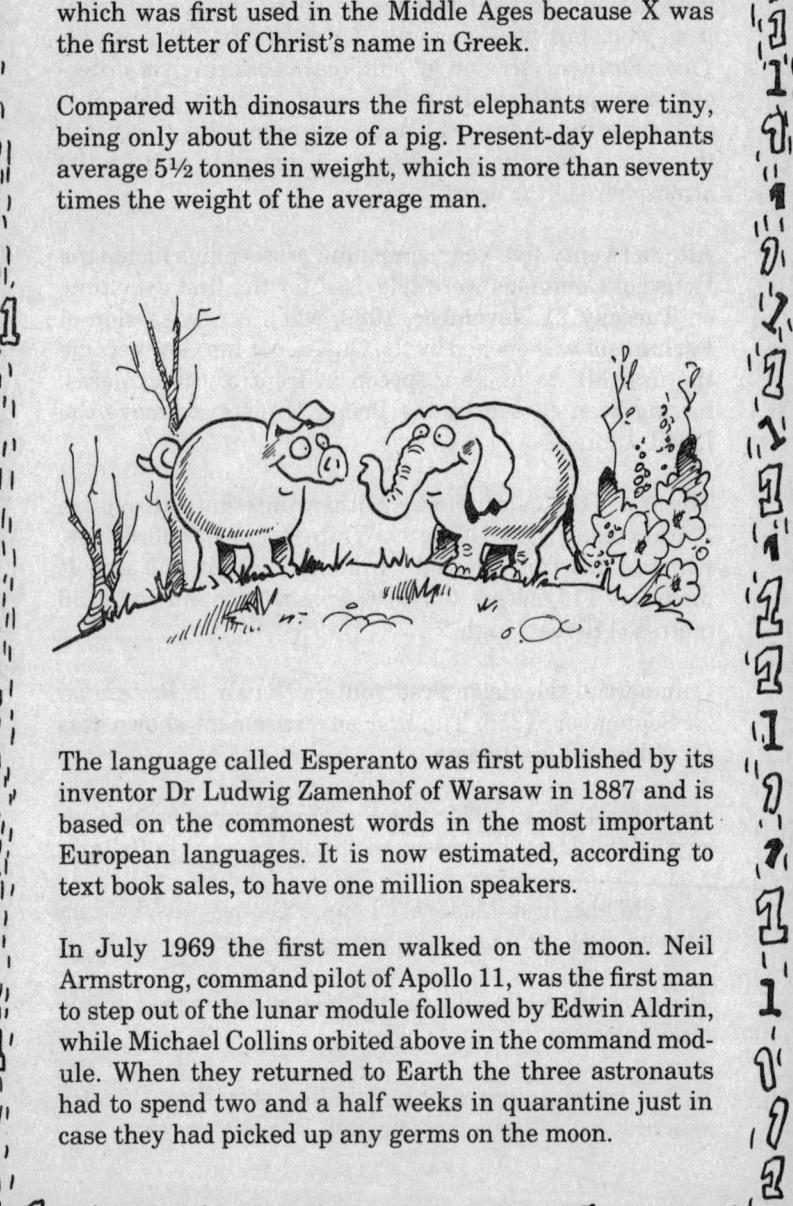

The language called Esperanto was first published by its inventor Dr Ludwig Zamenhof of Warsaw in 1887 and is based on the commonest words in the most important European languages. It is now estimated, according to text book sales, to have one million speakers.

In July 1969 the first men walked on the moon. Neil Armstrong, command pilot of Apollo 11, was the first man to step out of the lunar module followed by Edwin Aldrin, while Michael Collins orbited above in the command module. When they returned to Earth the three astronauts had to spend two and a half weeks in quarantine just in case they had picked up any germs on the moon.

ROYAL FIRSTS

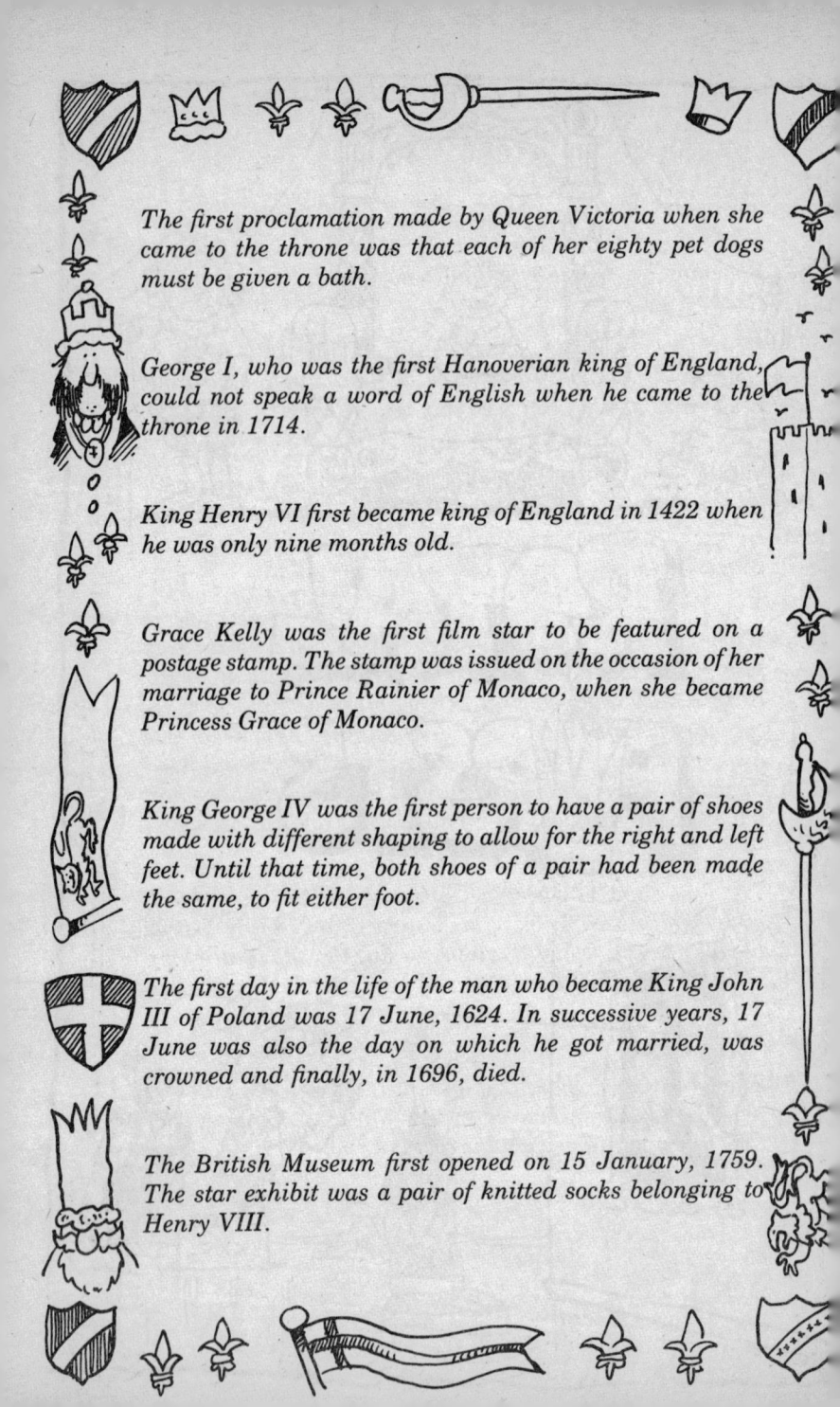

The first proclamation made by Queen Victoria when she came to the throne was that each of her eighty pet dogs must be given a bath.

George I, who was the first Hanoverian king of England, could not speak a word of English when he came to the throne in 1714.

King Henry VI first became king of England in 1422 when he was only nine months old.

Grace Kelly was the first film star to be featured on a postage stamp. The stamp was issued on the occasion of her marriage to Prince Rainier of Monaco, when she became Princess Grace of Monaco.

King George IV was the first person to have a pair of shoes made with different shaping to allow for the right and left feet. Until that time, both shoes of a pair had been made the same, to fit either foot.

The first day in the life of the man who became King John III of Poland was 17 June, 1624. In successive years, 17 June was also the day on which he got married, was crowned and finally, in 1696, died.

The British Museum first opened on 15 January, 1759. The star exhibit was a pair of knitted socks belonging to Henry VIII.

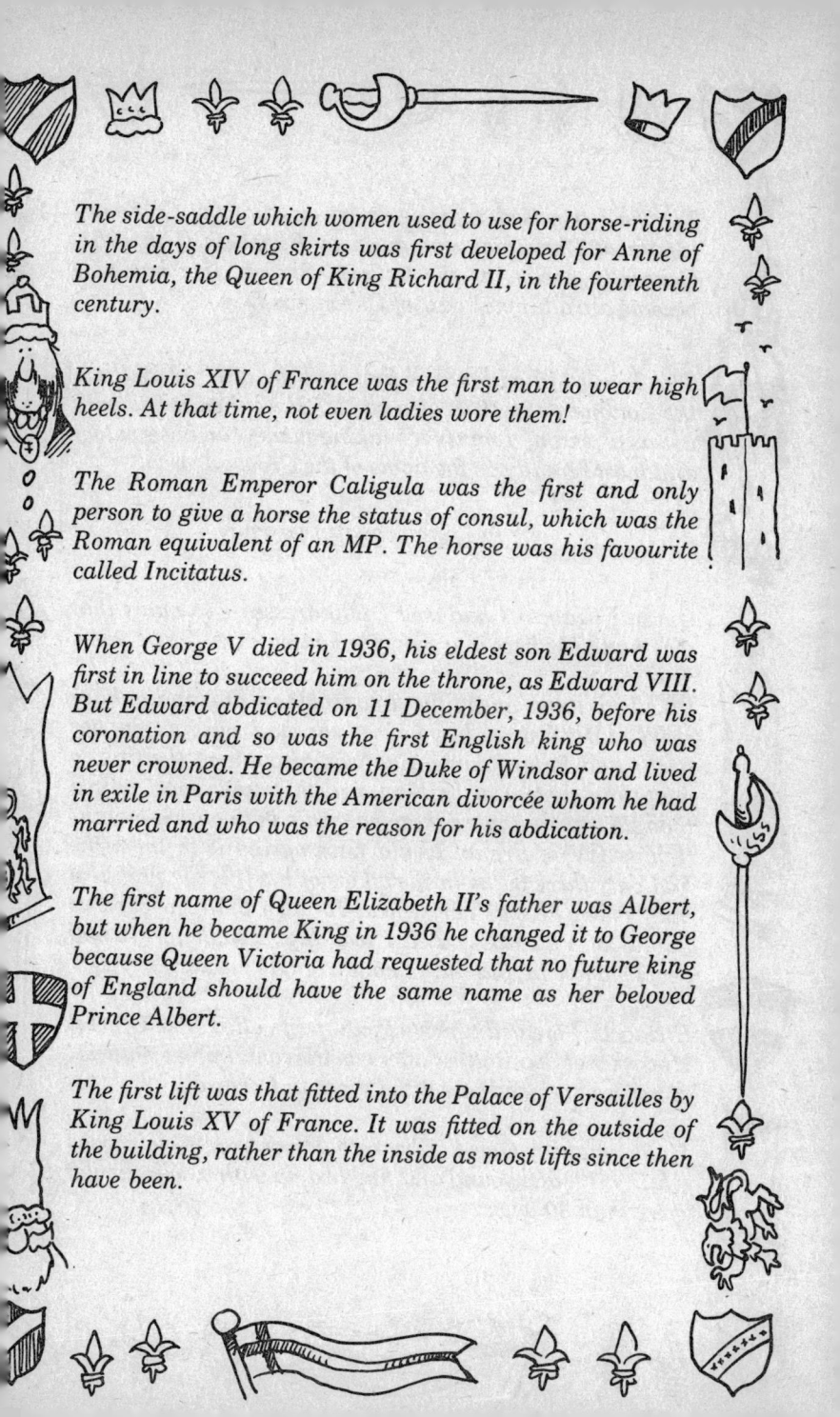

The side-saddle which women used to use for horse-riding in the days of long skirts was first developed for Anne of Bohemia, the Queen of King Richard II, in the fourteenth century.

King Louis XIV of France was the first man to wear high heels. At that time, not even ladies wore them!

The Roman Emperor Caligula was the first and only person to give a horse the status of consul, which was the Roman equivalent of an MP. The horse was his favourite called Incitatus.

When George V died in 1936, his eldest son Edward was first in line to succeed him on the throne, as Edward VIII. But Edward abdicated on 11 December, 1936, before his coronation and so was the first English king who was never crowned. He became the Duke of Windsor and lived in exile in Paris with the American divorcée whom he had married and who was the reason for his abdication.

The first name of Queen Elizabeth II's father was Albert, but when he became King in 1936 he changed it to George because Queen Victoria had requested that no future king of England should have the same name as her beloved Prince Albert.

The first lift was that fitted into the Palace of Versailles by King Louis XV of France. It was fitted on the outside of the building, rather than the inside as most lifts since then have been.

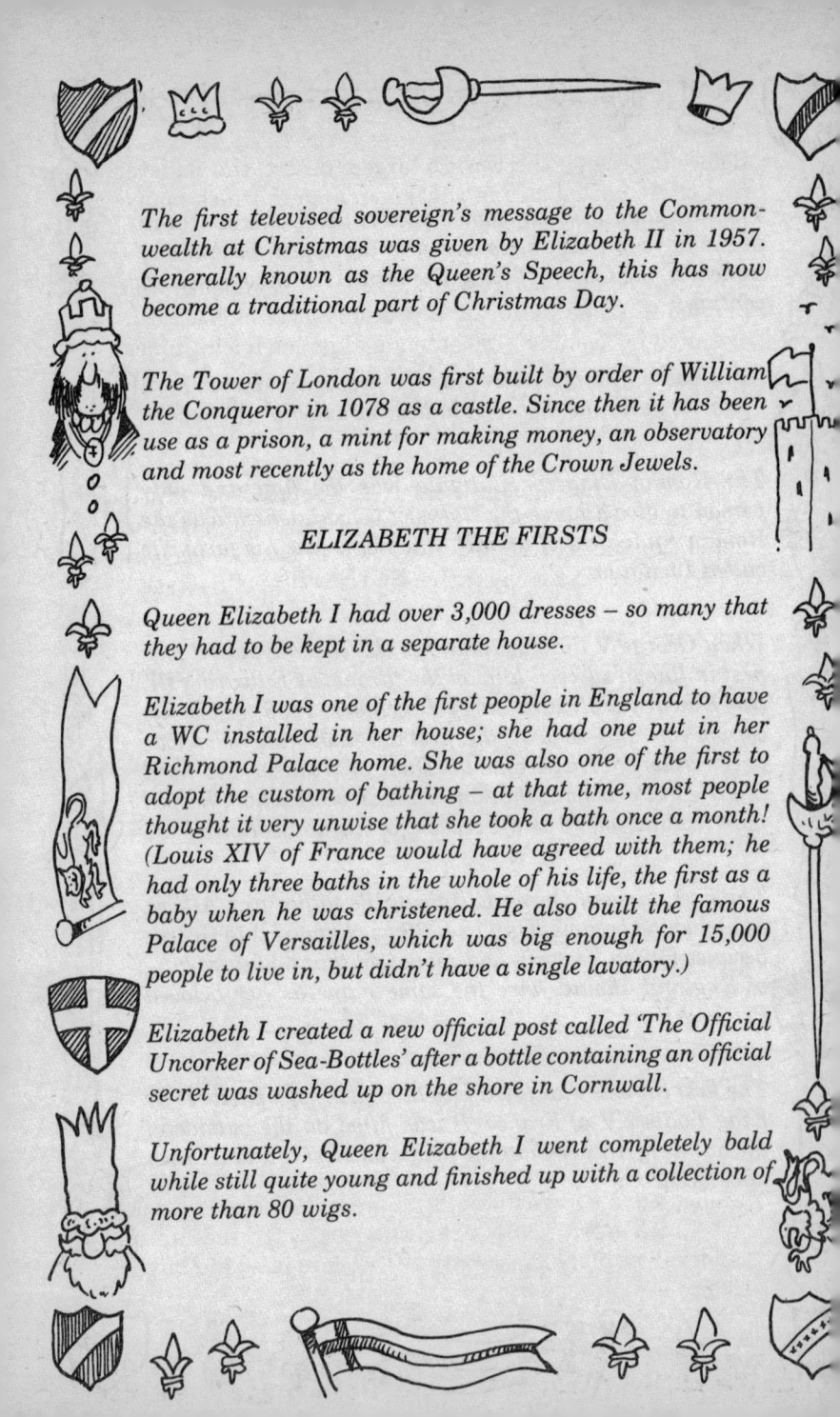

The first televised sovereign's message to the Commonwealth at Christmas was given by Elizabeth II in 1957. Generally known as the Queen's Speech, this has now become a traditional part of Christmas Day.

The Tower of London was first built by order of William the Conqueror in 1078 as a castle. Since then it has been use as a prison, a mint for making money, an observatory and most recently as the home of the Crown Jewels.

ELIZABETH THE FIRSTS

Queen Elizabeth I had over 3,000 dresses – so many that they had to be kept in a separate house.

Elizabeth I was one of the first people in England to have a WC installed in her house; she had one put in her Richmond Palace home. She was also one of the first to adopt the custom of bathing – at that time, most people thought it very unwise that she took a bath once a month! (Louis XIV of France would have agreed with them; he had only three baths in the whole of his life, the first as a baby when he was christened. He also built the famous Palace of Versailles, which was big enough for 15,000 people to live in, but didn't have a single lavatory.)

Elizabeth I created a new official post called 'The Official Uncorker of Sea-Bottles' after a bottle containing an official secret was washed up on the shore in Cornwall.

Unfortunately, Queen Elizabeth I went completely bald while still quite young and finished up with a collection of more than 80 wigs.

Before it became the world's largest desert, the Sahara first of all existed as a fertile, green area in which many plants and animals lived.

The first and only portrait of the Duke of Monmouth was painted when he was dead. It was only after he had been executed for leading a rebellion against his uncle James II that it was realised that he had never sat for a portrait. His head was quickly stitched back on and his portrait painted. That portrait now hangs in the National Gallery.

The first successful expedition to the South Pole, which took place in 1911, was led by the Norwegian explorer Roald Amundsen, who had also five years earlier been in charge of the first navigation of the North-west Passage.

An American scientist called Charles Towney built the world's first laser in 1960. The word 'laser' stands for Light Amplification by Stimulated Emission of Radiation.

In June 1957 the first Premium Bond draw took place. The machine that is used to generate the winning numbers is called Ernie, which stands for Electronic Random Number Indicator Equipment.

Monasteries were first so called because the first monks were men who wanted to live solitary lives and so withdrew into their shelter to live alone. *Monos* in Greek means 'alone'.

The first time that the number of motor vehicles in Britain topped the one million mark was in 1923. Today there are in the region of twenty million vehicles in the country.

The Russian cosmonaut Yuri Gagarin was the first man to complete a successful flight in space. He achieved this feat on 12 April, 1961. Tragically, he was killed in a low-level jet plane crash only a few years later in March 1968.

A ballad written in 1559 is the first known instance of the saying 'The nearer the bone, the sweeter the meat'.

Easter Island in the Pacific Ocean got its name because it was first discovered on Easter Day in 1722.

The world's first dry dock for repairing ships was put into service in Portsmouth in 1496.

On 25 July, 1909 Louis Blériot became the first man to fly an aeroplane across the Channel from England to France. His journey took him thirty-seven minutes.

When it was first invented, porridge was not the cereal dish we know it as today, but a thick vegetable soup.

Alaska first became part of the United States of America in 1959. It is by far the largest state, being more than twice the size of Texas which had had the distinction of being the largest state until that time.

The custom of toasting someone with a glass of wine first began as a result of pieces of toast being put into drinks to improve their flavour. This habit led to the idea of toasting someone to indicate that he is felt to add to the 'flavour' of things.

Red was the colour of the first known dye. It was obtained from a Middle Eastern shrub 4,000 years ago.

The first and only English Pope, Nicholas Breakspear, died in an unlikely manner. He had the misfortune to swallow a fly in a glass of wine and choked to death.

Parking meters were invented by an American, Carl M. Magee, and were first installed in Oklahoma City in July 1935. Traffic wardens first appeared much more recently, in 1964.

The 1p and 2p decimal coins were first issued on 15 January, 1971. The British decimal currency system replaced the old pounds, shillings and pence on 15 February of that year.

The word 'palace' has its origin in Roman times. It is based on the name Palatine Hill, which is one of the seven hills on which Rome was built and the hill where many of the Roman Emperors had their grand houses, or palaces.

A Frenchman called Denis Papin designed the first pressure cooker in 1680.

The first hot-air balloon World Championships took place in Albuquerque, New Mexico, USA in February 1973.

The first ever marathon runner collapsed and died as a result of his efforts. He ran 40 kilometres to the city of Athens to carry news of the victory over the Persians at the Battle of Marathon and to issue a warning that the Persians were sailing down the coast to launch another attack. In those days messengers carrying *bad* news were often slain so it was particularly unlucky for this messenger that he died from the process of carrying *good* news.

The first electric toothbrush was manufactured by the Squibb Company of New York in 1961.

In AD 982 Eric the Red discovered the largest island in the world and called it Greenland. He chose the name deliberately because the island was cold and barren with ice covering more than three-quarters of its surface, but he wanted his fellow Norsemen to think it was a green and pleasant place to settle. Twenty-five ships full of settlers set sail immediately for the 'green land'.

Kaleidoscopes were invented in 1816 for the use of textile designers. It was incidental that they became popular as toys.

One of the most difficult-to-solve 'puzzles' ever produced, the Rubik cube, was invented in 1975 by Professor Erno Rubik of Budapest. The cube was first produced for the mass market in 1979.

The first boxes of assorted chocolates were produced in Britain by Cadbury's in 1866.

The Pyramids were faced with marble when they were first built.

Although chop suey is thought of as a dish originating from China, it was first created in New York in 1896 by a Chinese ambassador's chef using a hotch-potch of ingredients. The dish was not known in China at that time.

In 1852 the first public lavatory opened in London. People were used to managing without this convenience – it was only used on eighty-two occasions in the whole of the first month!

SPORTING FYRSTS

he's trying fly fishing!

...but he can't get the <u>hook</u> to stay up in the <u>air</u>!

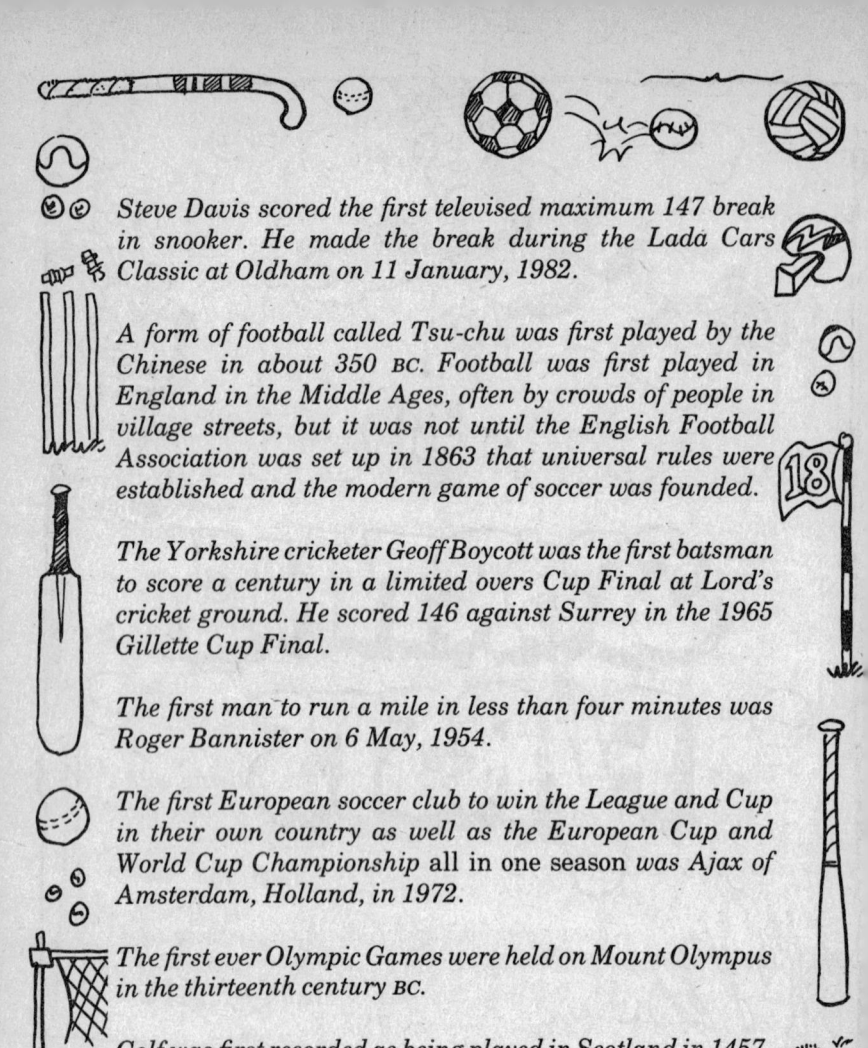

Steve Davis scored the first televised maximum 147 break in snooker. He made the break during the Lada Cars Classic at Oldham on 11 January, 1982.

A form of football called Tsu-chu was first played by the Chinese in about 350 BC. Football was first played in England in the Middle Ages, often by crowds of people in village streets, but it was not until the English Football Association was set up in 1863 that universal rules were established and the modern game of soccer was founded.

The Yorkshire cricketer Geoff Boycott was the first batsman to score a century in a limited overs Cup Final at Lord's cricket ground. He scored 146 against Surrey in the 1965 Gillette Cup Final.

The first man to run a mile in less than four minutes was Roger Bannister on 6 May, 1954.

The first European soccer club to win the League and Cup in their own country as well as the European Cup and World Cup Championship all in one season was Ajax of Amsterdam, Holland, in 1972.

The first ever Olympic Games were held on Mount Olympus in the thirteenth century BC.

Golf was first recorded as being played in Scotland in 1457.

In American football, the first Super Bowl contest was held in 1967. The biggest number of wins of this annual event is four, by the Pittsburgh Steelers.

The first person to become an international sports player at only eight years old was Joy Foster, who was the Jamaican singles and mixed doubles table tennis champion in 1958.

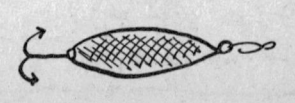

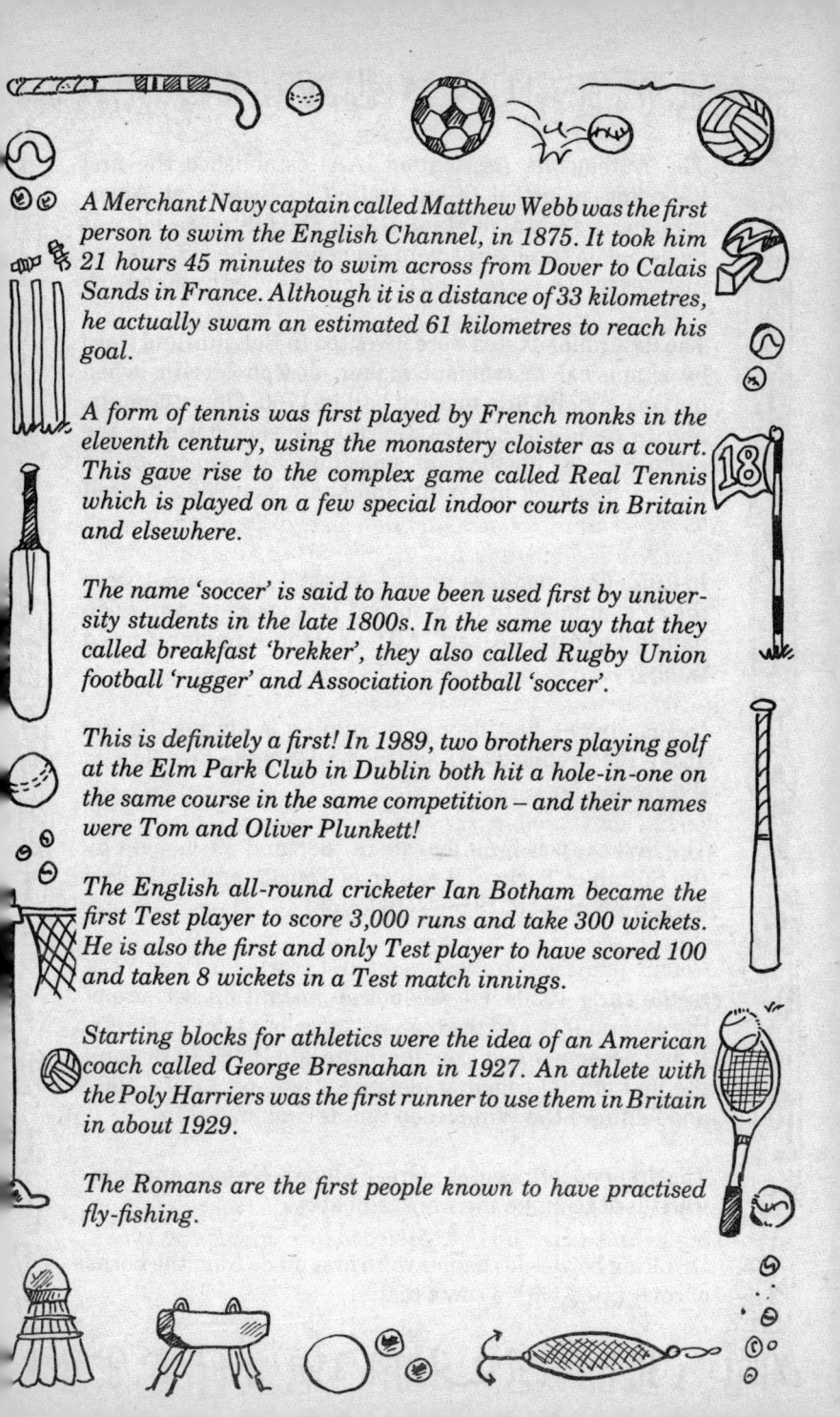

A Merchant Navy captain called Matthew Webb was the first person to swim the English Channel, in 1875. It took him 21 hours 45 minutes to swim across from Dover to Calais Sands in France. Although it is a distance of 33 kilometres, he actually swam an estimated 61 kilometres to reach his goal.

A form of tennis was first played by French monks in the eleventh century, using the monastery cloister as a court. This gave rise to the complex game called Real Tennis which is played on a few special indoor courts in Britain and elsewhere.

The name 'soccer' is said to have been used first by university students in the late 1800s. In the same way that they called breakfast 'brekker', they also called Rugby Union football 'rugger' and Association football 'soccer'.

This is definitely a first! In 1989, two brothers playing golf at the Elm Park Club in Dublin both hit a hole-in-one on the same course in the same competition – and their names were Tom and Oliver Plunkett!

The English all-round cricketer Ian Botham became the first Test player to score 3,000 runs and take 300 wickets. He is also the first and only Test player to have scored 100 and taken 8 wickets in a Test match innings.

Starting blocks for athletics were the idea of an American coach called George Bresnahan in 1927. An athlete with the Poly Harriers was the first runner to use them in Britain in about 1929.

The Romans are the first people known to have practised fly-fishing.

The Automobile Association (AA) established the first bulk-storage petrol filling station in Britain at Aldermaston, Berkshire in March 1920. The filling station was modelled on those already in existence in the USA. It was manned by AA patrols and could only be used by members.

The first roller skates were invented in Belgium and worn by a musical instrument maker, Joseph Merlin, when playing a violin at a masked ball in 1760. Unfortunately, Merlin could not change direction or slow down on the skates, so he finished up smashing into an expensive mirror, breaking his violin and badly wounding himself as well.

In 1951 four monkeys named Albert 1, 2, 3, and 4 were the first animals to be launched into space in a mission named 'Operation Albert'. All four of the animals returned safely.

In Britain the first floor of a building is always the one above the ground floor, but in the USA the first floor *is* the ground floor.

The first car was built for sale in 1888 and was bought by the Sultan of Turkey. It ran on electricity and could do a maximum speed of 10 mph (16 kmph).

Colour television transmission first started in New York in the early 1950s but was not an instant hit because of the poor quality and the high cost of colour television sets. It first became widely popular in the late 1960s. In Britain, the first official colour transmission was on 1 July, 1967 and featured the Wimbledon tennis championships.

The first two letters of the Greek alphabet, *alpha* and *beta*, were used to make the word 'alphabet'.

Drinking bottles for babies were first made from the horns of cows fitted with a cow's teat.

Research has shown that more people develop colds on the first working day of the week, Monday, than on any other day.

The first national museum in England was the British Museum opened in 1753. In those days you could not go in automatically but had to apply for permission, which took about two weeks and was only given if the authorities approved of you.

The first 'test-tube' baby, Louise Brown, was born on 25 July, 1978. Patrick Steptoe and Dr Robert Edwards created history when they successfully fertilised a human egg in the laboratory and implanted it back into the mother.

The first major international fair was the Great Exhibition of 1851, which took place in the Crystal Palace built in Hyde Park, London. More than six million people visited the fair in the space of 141 days.

The Greeks were the first people to think of making beds comfortable. They fitted strips of leather across their beds to make them more springy.

The word 'noon' for 12 midday first came from the Latin *nonus* meaning nine. This is because the Romans first started their clock at 6 a.m. in the morning by the time we use now, so their ninth hour was 3 p.m. by our clock and is the mid-point between sunset and sunrise at midsummer.

On 19 September, 1897 a taxi-driver called George Smith became the first British motorist to be convicted of drunken driving.

The seventeenth-century writer John Dryden was the first official Poet Laureate in England.

In 1879 the first Woolworth's store opened in New York State, USA. The shop was established by Frank Winfield Woolworth and based on the fact that nothing on display would cost more than five cents (less than 10p).

Alice Wells became the first policewoman in the world in September 1910 when she joined the police force in Los Angeles, USA.

When the planet Uranus was first discovered it was called *Georgium Sidium* after King George III of England.

British passenger trains have first- and second-class carriages. But at first, before 3 June, 1956 when they were scrapped, there were also third-class carriages.

When the First World War started there were only fifty men in the American air force.

The Phoenicians are thought to have been the first to sail around Africa, 600 years before the birth of Christ.

Volcanoes were first so-called after Vulcan, the Roman god of fire.

Old-age pensions were first started in Britain in 1908.

In Iceland people are listed in telephone directories by their first names rather than their surnames as in Britain.

The early Olympic games were very unlike those held nowadays. In AD 60 the Roman Emperor Nero, who was one of the worst athletes ever to compete in the games, took the first prize in every event because he himself was in charge of awarding the prizes!

LITERARY FIRSTS

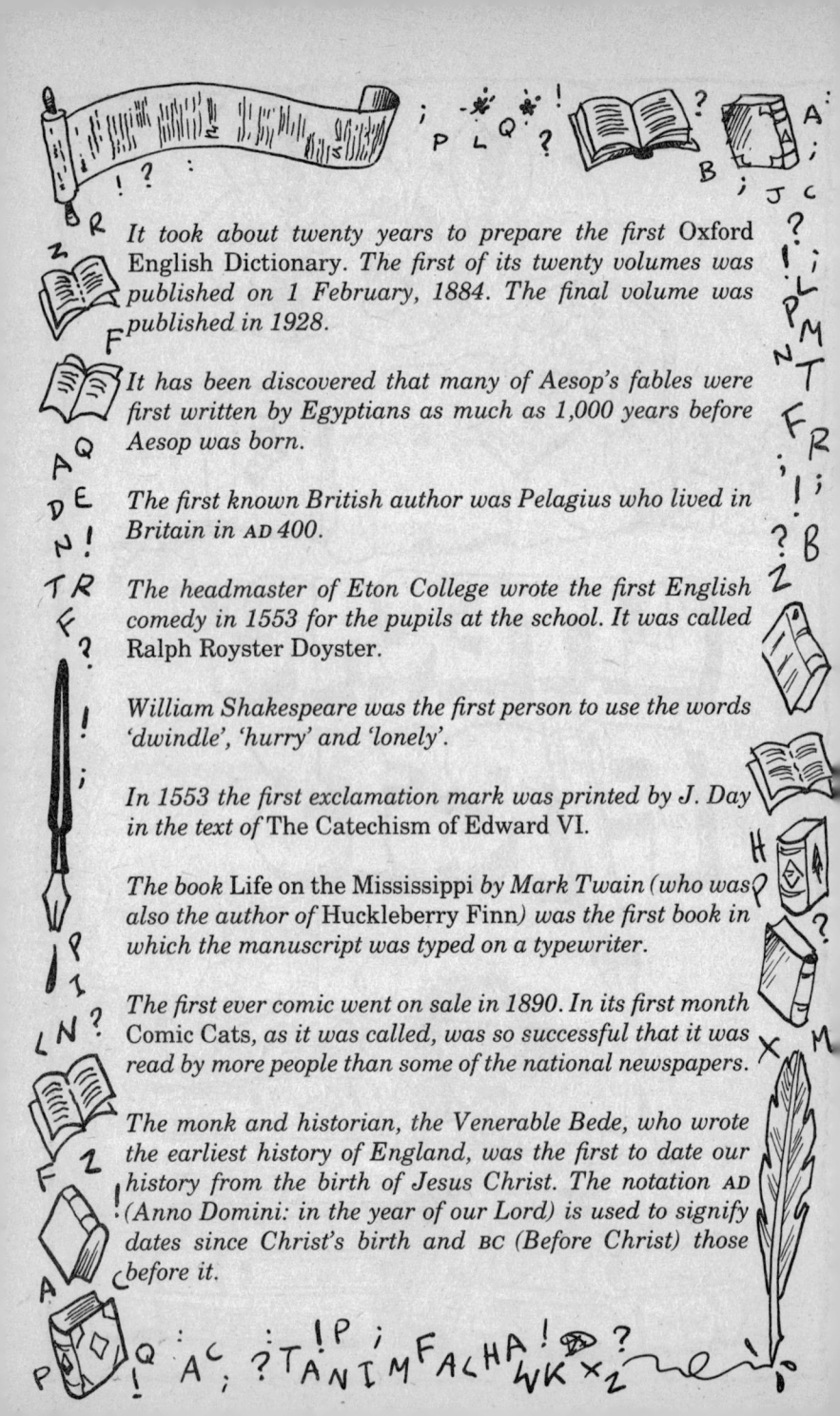

It took about twenty years to prepare the first Oxford English Dictionary. The first of its twenty volumes was published on 1 February, 1884. The final volume was published in 1928.

It has been discovered that many of Aesop's fables were first written by Egyptians as much as 1,000 years before Aesop was born.

The first known British author was Pelagius who lived in Britain in AD 400.

The headmaster of Eton College wrote the first English comedy in 1553 for the pupils at the school. It was called Ralph Royster Doyster.

William Shakespeare was the first person to use the words 'dwindle', 'hurry' and 'lonely'.

In 1553 the first exclamation mark was printed by J. Day in the text of The Catechism of Edward VI.

The book Life on the Mississippi by Mark Twain (who was also the author of Huckleberry Finn) was the first book in which the manuscript was typed on a typewriter.

The first ever comic went on sale in 1890. In its first month Comic Cats, as it was called, was so successful that it was read by more people than some of the national newspapers.

The monk and historian, the Venerable Bede, who wrote the earliest history of England, was the first to date our history from the birth of Jesus Christ. The notation AD (Anno Domini: in the year of our Lord) is used to signify dates since Christ's birth and BC (Before Christ) those before it.

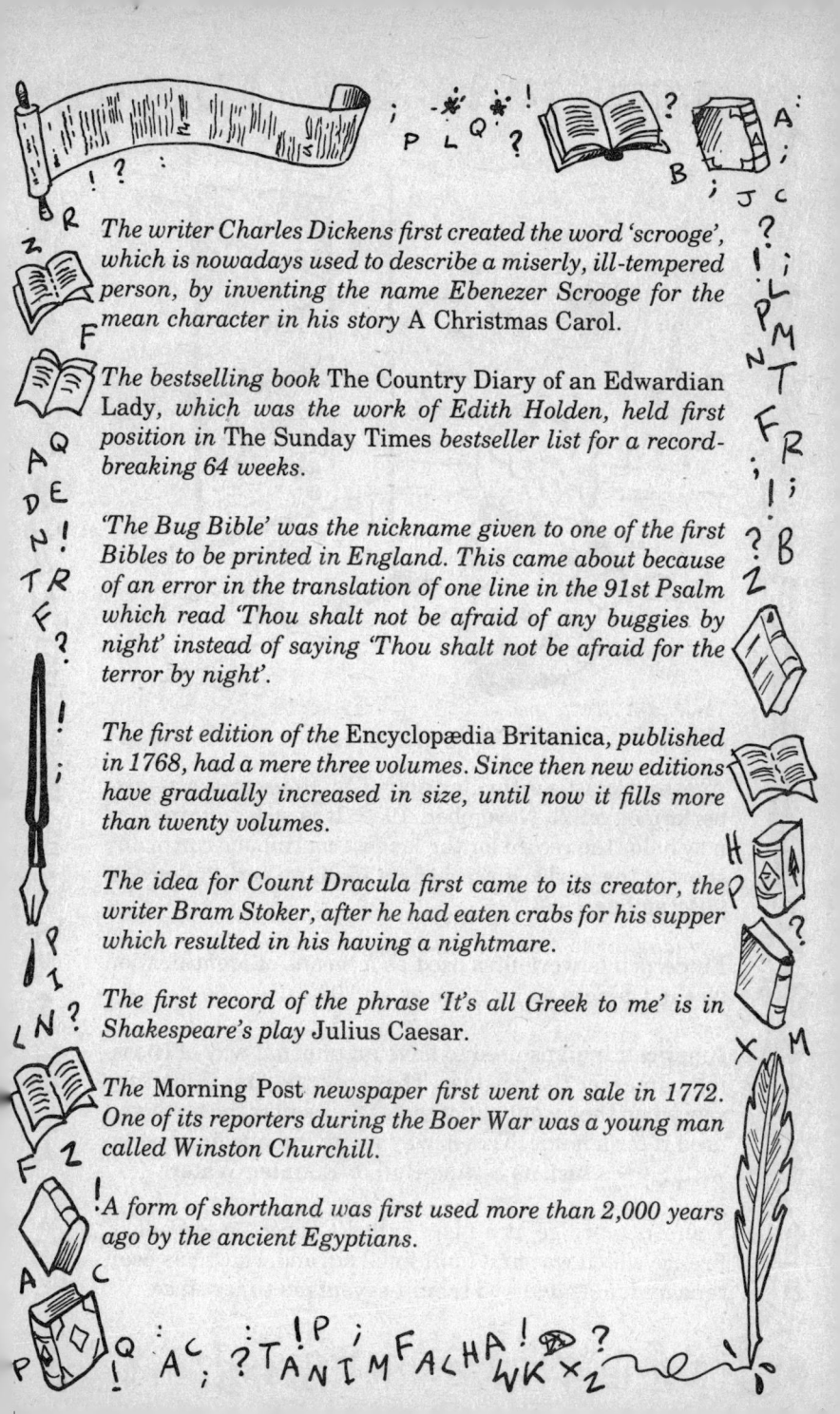

The writer Charles Dickens first created the word 'scrooge', which is nowadays used to describe a miserly, ill-tempered person, by inventing the name Ebenezer Scrooge for the mean character in his story A Christmas Carol.

The bestselling book The Country Diary of an Edwardian Lady, which was the work of Edith Holden, held first position in The Sunday Times bestseller list for a record-breaking 64 weeks.

'The Bug Bible' was the nickname given to one of the first Bibles to be printed in England. This came about because of an error in the translation of one line in the 91st Psalm which read 'Thou shalt not be afraid of any buggies by night' instead of saying 'Thou shalt not be afraid for the terror by night'.

The first edition of the Encyclopædia Britanica, published in 1768, had a mere three volumes. Since then new editions have gradually increased in size, until now it fills more than twenty volumes.

The idea for Count Dracula first came to its creator, the writer Bram Stoker, after he had eaten crabs for his supper which resulted in his having a nightmare.

The first record of the phrase 'It's all Greek to me' is in Shakespeare's play Julius Caesar.

The Morning Post newspaper first went on sale in 1772. One of its reporters during the Boer War was a young man called Winston Churchill.

A form of shorthand was first used more than 2,000 years ago by the ancient Egyptians.

Agatha Christie's thriller play *The Mousetrap* was first performed on 25 November, 1952. It is still running and now holds the record for the longest continuous run of any show in the world. It reached its 15,000th performance on 9 December, 1988.

Fingerprints were first used as a means of identification by the Chinese as long ago as AD 700.

American Indians used to have an unusual way of choosing names for their babies. They took the first thing they saw when they went out of their tepees after the birth and used it for a name. This is why many Indians finished up with names such as Sitting Bull or Running Water.

There is a bridge at a place called Charenton-le-Pont in France which was first built in 52 BC, and which has been rendered unusable and rebuilt seventeen times since.

Karate, the form of self-defence in which only hands, elbows, knees and feet are used, appeared in Japan for the first time in 1916. It was developed on the Pacific island of Okinawa, south-west of Japan.

The first land animals developed from creatures that had originated in the sea.

Aluminium was first used by man only a century ago even though it is one of the most common metals in the Earth's crust.

On 4 October, 1957 the first satellite was launched into space by the Russians. It was called *Sputnik I*.

The ancient Spaniards, or Moors, were probably the first to do morris dancing or, as it was called, Moorish dancing.

The first five of the highest volcanoes in the world are all in the South American Andes, which is the longest range of mountains in the world.

On 3 December, 1967 the first human heart transplant operation was performed in Cape Town, South Africa, by Professor Christiaan Barnard with a team of thirty doctors and nurses. The fifty-five-year-old patient lived for eighteen days after the operation. Britain's first heart transplant took place on 3 May, 1968 and the patient survived for forty-six days.

The first glass is thought to have originated from Egypt around 1500 BC. Glass-blowing dates from the first century AD.

The world's first launderette was opened in the USA in 1934.

The verb to 'nag' first came from the Anglo-Saxon word 'gnagan' which meant to chew or bite.

For centuries builders have been using mortar to hold bricks and stones together but it was only in 1824 that modern Portland cement was first used.

Hallmarks are stamped on precious metals to show they are of a certain standard of purity. Silver was first hallmarked in the fourteenth century but platinum, which is also a precious metal, has only been hallmarked since 1974.

The stretch of water separating Alaska and Siberia was first discovered by the Danish sailor, Vitus Bering, and as a result is called the Bering Strait.

The first European to find the sea route to the Far East by sailing round the Cape of Good Hope at the southern tip of Africa was Vasco da Gama from Portugal. Until the building of the Suez Canal in the nineteenth century, this was the only way of sailing to India from Europe.

One of the first known methods of teeth cleaning was that used by the early Spaniards. They found that teeth could be cleaned successfully with urine!

The shipping distress call 'Mayday' originated in the first place from the French *m'aidez*, which means 'help me'.

In horse-riding, to move at a fairly fast speed is called to 'canter'. This word was first used because the Pilgrims used to ride their horses fairly fast to reach the shrine of Thomas à Becket at Canterbury.

When Sir Charles Napier's troops won the battle of Hyderabad in 1843, the first thing he did was to inform headquarters of the good news by sending a message that read simply *peccavi*. This is the Latin for 'I have sinned', which he used as a clever play on words because Hyderabad is in the state of Sind.

The first recorded eclipse of the sun was in China in 781 BC.

Since records first began in 1623, twenty-two meteorites are known to have fallen on the British Isles, the heaviest of which, weighing at least 46.25 kilograms fell in Leicestershire on 24 December, 1965.

The first perfumes were created from burnt wood and gums mixed with herbs, and the word perfume was used to describe them because it actually means 'through smoke'.

Charles Dickens first wrote his novels in the form of serials.

The modern-sounding expression 'Right on' actually appeared for the first time in the play *Julius Caesar* written in the sixteenth century by William Shakespeare.

Christmas crackers first originated in Victorian times. A London baker and confectioner, Tom Smith, claimed to have invented crackers, developing them as fun-packaging for the bon-bons he sold. The first known illustration of a cracker is that in the Christmas 1847 issue of the *Illustrated London News*.

Hanging beds called hammocks were first used by Indians living in the Caribbean. Later they became popular with sailors who found them good for sleeping in on board ships.

Butterflies were at first called 'flutterbies'.

The world's first restaurant was opened in Madrid in 1725.

The first needles for sewing were made of bone about 30,000 years ago. Animal sinews were used as the first 'thread'.

The first name of a pub in Westcott, Devon, was the shortest name of any pub in Britain. But in October 1983 the 'X', as it was called, had its name changed to the 'Merry Harriers'.

Fragments of the first known canals in the world were found near Mandali, Iraq, in 1968. They have been dated to about 4,000 BC.

FAST FIRSTS

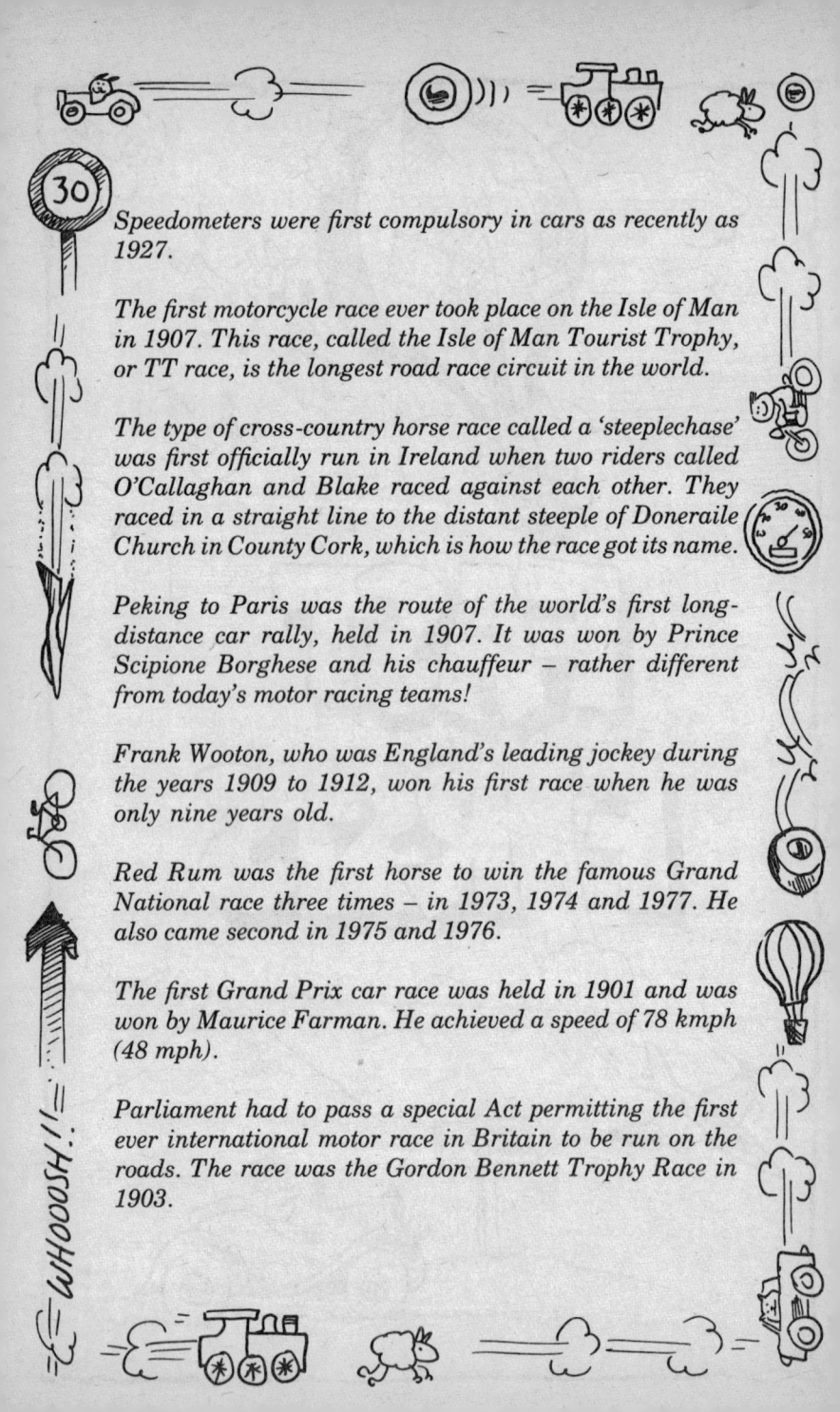

Speedometers were first compulsory in cars as recently as 1927.

The first motorcycle race ever took place on the Isle of Man in 1907. This race, called the Isle of Man Tourist Trophy, or TT race, is the longest road race circuit in the world.

The type of cross-country horse race called a 'steeplechase' was first officially run in Ireland when two riders called O'Callaghan and Blake raced against each other. They raced in a straight line to the distant steeple of Doneraile Church in County Cork, which is how the race got its name.

Peking to Paris was the route of the world's first long-distance car rally, held in 1907. It was won by Prince Scipione Borghese and his chauffeur – rather different from today's motor racing teams!

Frank Wooton, who was England's leading jockey during the years 1909 to 1912, won his first race when he was only nine years old.

Red Rum was the first horse to win the famous Grand National race three times – in 1973, 1974 and 1977. He also came second in 1975 and 1976.

The first Grand Prix car race was held in 1901 and was won by Maurice Farman. He achieved a speed of 78 kmph (48 mph).

Parliament had to pass a special Act permitting the first ever international motor race in Britain to be run on the roads. The race was the Gordon Bennett Trophy Race in 1903.

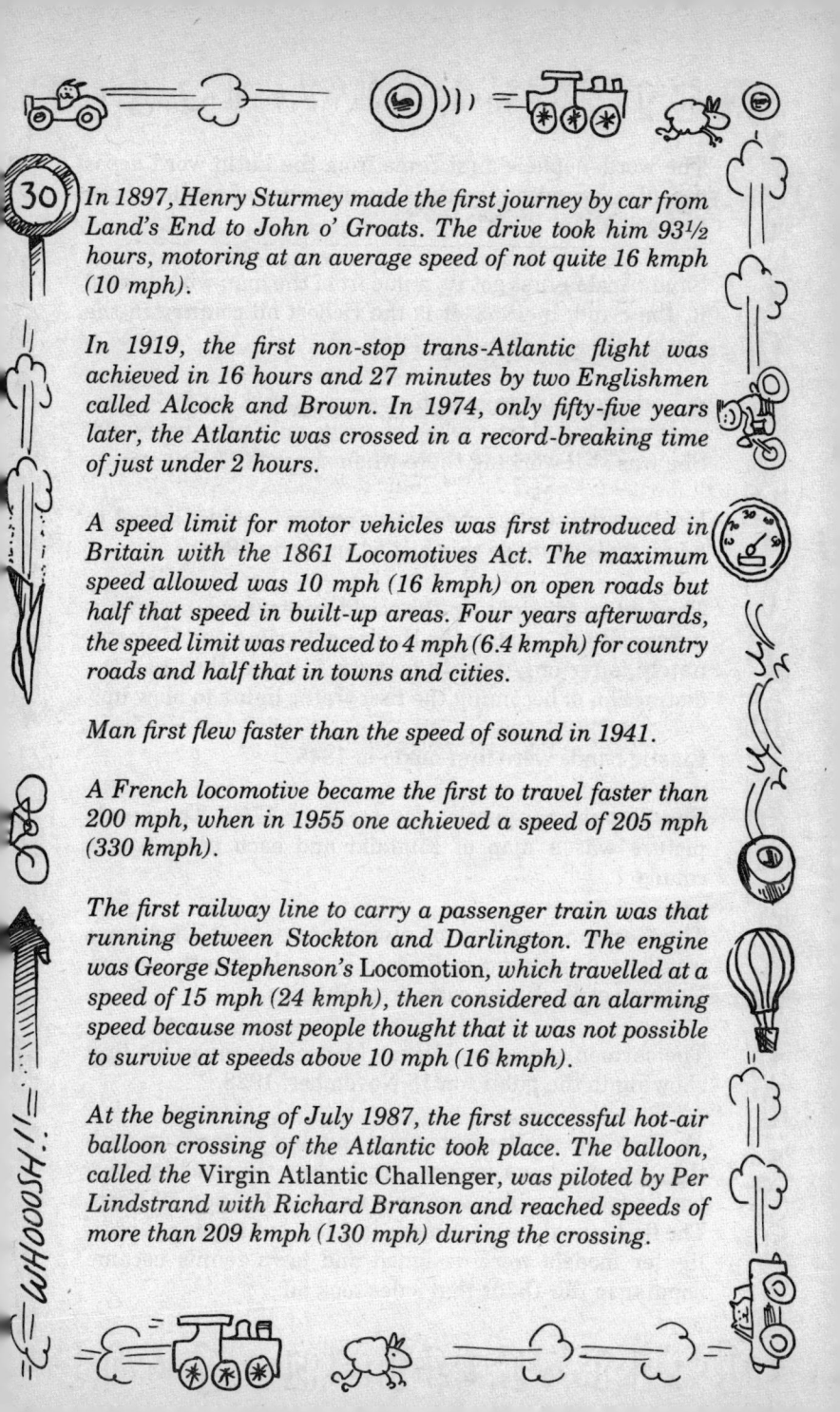

In 1897, Henry Sturmey made the first journey by car from Land's End to John o' Groats. The drive took him 93½ hours, motoring at an average speed of not quite 16 kmph (10 mph).

In 1919, the first non-stop trans-Atlantic flight was achieved in 16 hours and 27 minutes by two Englishmen called Alcock and Brown. In 1974, only fifty-five years later, the Atlantic was crossed in a record-breaking time of just under 2 hours.

A speed limit for motor vehicles was first introduced in Britain with the 1861 Locomotives Act. The maximum speed allowed was 10 mph (16 kmph) on open roads but half that speed in built-up areas. Four years afterwards, the speed limit was reduced to 4 mph (6.4 kmph) for country roads and half that in towns and cities.

Man first flew faster than the speed of sound in 1941.

A French locomotive became the first to travel faster than 200 mph, when in 1955 one achieved a speed of 205 mph (330 kmph).

The first railway line to carry a passenger train was that running between Stockton and Darlington. The engine was George Stephenson's Locomotion, which travelled at a speed of 15 mph (24 kmph), then considered an alarming speed because most people thought that it was not possible to survive at speeds above 10 mph (16 kmph).

At the beginning of July 1987, the first successful hot-air balloon crossing of the Atlantic took place. The balloon, called the Virgin Atlantic Challenger, was piloted by Per Lindstrand with Richard Branson and reached speeds of more than 209 kmph (130 mph) during the crossing.

The word 'nephew' first came from the Latin word *nepos* meaning grandson, so the first meaning of nephew is in fact grandson. Phew!

Saudi Arabia first got its name from the man who created it, Ibn Saud, in 1953. It is the richest oil country in the world.

A Leicestershire woman first started working for a company making elastic when she was only nine years old. She was still working there when she was 95.

Marlborough College was the first boys' public school to admit girls. It made this historic move in 1968.

The first traffic lights in the world were placed in a prominent position – outside the Houses of Parliament. Unfortunately, after only twenty-four days in use, they had the distinction of becoming the first traffic lights to blow up.

Elastic bands were first made in 1845.

The first jigsaw puzzle was made in 1767. The puzzle picture was a map of England and each piece was a county.

The German tradition of giving presents at Christmas was first introduced to Britain by a nineteenth-century Duchess of York who came from Russia.

The cartoon character Mickey Mouse was given his first showing to the public on 18 November, 1928.

Mr Budding of Gloucester was the first to come up with the idea of a lawn mower, inspired by the machine in a textile factory which was able to shear the nap off cloth. The first machines were made in 1830, but it was not until lighter models were designed and lawn tennis became popular in the 1870s that sales took off.

The first prize for improvisation in the natural world must go to the chaffinch which made its entire nest out of confetti!

The first ever Test Match was won by England against Australia at the Oval cricket ground in 1880.

The word 'million' was first used in 1370.

Parachutes were first invented to help people jump to safety when they were trapped inside burning buildings. Their use in jumping from aeroplanes came much later as aeroplanes were not invented for another hundred years.

When an ant wakes up it first stretches and then often yawns!

The first hotel in which each room was supplied with a bathroom was opened in Boston, America, in 1829. But 'mod. cons.' were still a long way off, for the bathrooms were not even on the same floor as the bedrooms.

Jeans were first made by a man called Levi Strauss for workers who needed tough clothing when they were digging in California during the Gold Rush.

The first day of the twentieth century was not 1 January 1900, but 1 January 1901.

The term 'silly billy' was first used by William, Duke of Gloucester in referring to his cousin King William IV.

The use of guide dogs to help blind people first started because of the actions of an alsatian dog belonging to a German doctor. Dr Gorlitz used to walk in his hospital's grounds with one of his patients who was partially paralysed. But one day he was called away and had to leave the patient to manage on his own. When the doctor returned he saw that his dog had fetched the patient's walking stick and was leading him safely back.

The first decoration awarded for bravery was the laurel wreath used in the time of the ancient Greeks and Romans. But the great Roman general Julius Caesar nearly always wore a laurel wreath because he used it to hide his baldness.

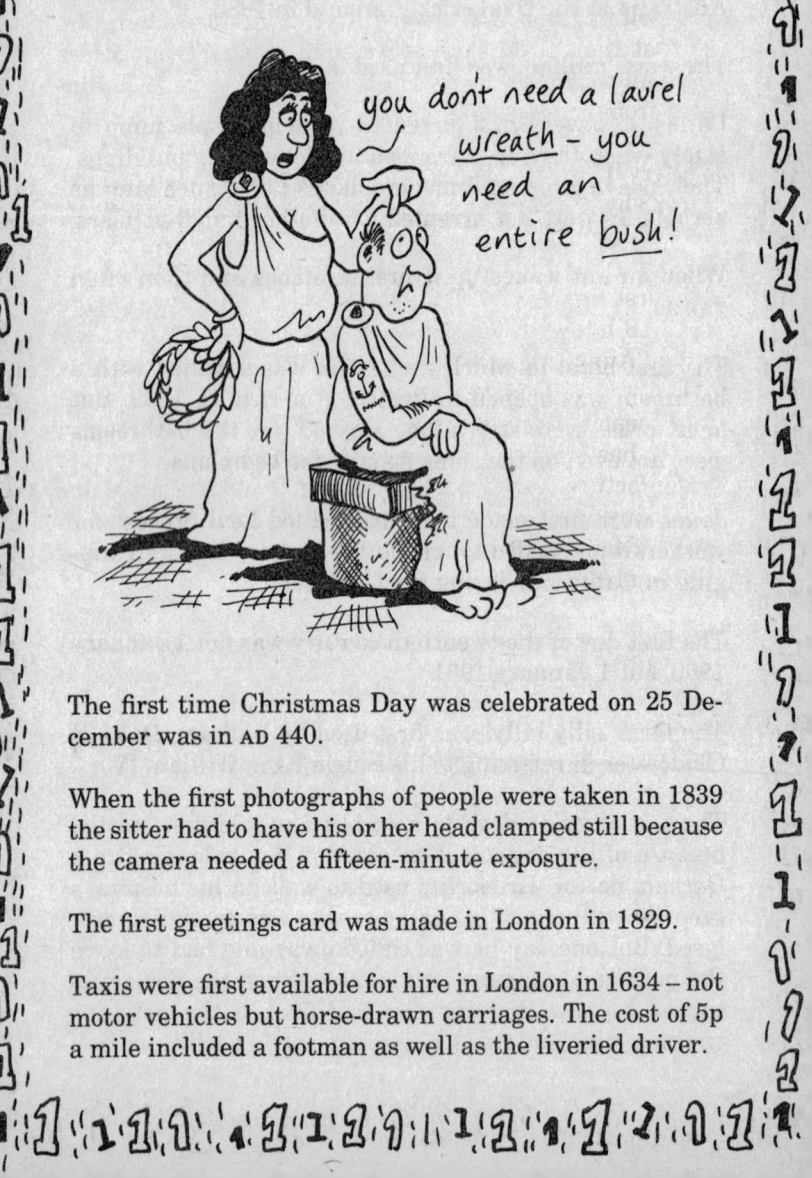

you don't need a laurel wreath — you need an entire bush!

The first time Christmas Day was celebrated on 25 December was in AD 440.

When the first photographs of people were taken in 1839 the sitter had to have his or her head clamped still because the camera needed a fifteen-minute exposure.

The first greetings card was made in London in 1829.

Taxis were first available for hire in London in 1634 – not motor vehicles but horse-drawn carriages. The cost of 5p a mile included a footman as well as the liveried driver.

The first fingerprints were made in 1858 but it was not until 1880 that their use in solving crimes was first realised. A century later, in 1989, the use of fingerprints in fighting crime was taken a stage further with an experiment in Leicestershire. For the first time, do-it-yourself fingerprint kits were given to victims of burglars so that they could save police time by supplying prints from all people on the premises who could then be eliminated from enquiries.

The cry 'Hip, hip, hooray' was first shouted as long ago as AD 638 by the Saracens, or Arabs, when they captured the city of Jerusalem.

The first fire-engine of which there is a record was made in 1518 by a goldsmith called Anthony Blatner for the city of Augsburg in Germany.

The meat substitute called Textured Vegetable Protein (TVP) has its origin in the car industry! The idea for its manufacture first came to Robert Boyer of the Ford Motor Company while he was searching for an alternative to leather for car upholstery. He discovered that a kind of artificial 'meat' could be spun from soya fibres.

The 999 emergency telephone service was first introduced on 1 July, 1937.

It first became possible to telephone New York from London in January 1927. The cost was £15 for three minutes, surprisingly similar to the charge made today.

The reason that people talk about 'unravelling' the clues of a mystery is because the first meaning of a clue or 'clew' was a ball of thread or rope.

The salt mine in Wieliczka, Poland, is believed to be one of the first ever dug. It has been in operation for nearly 1,000 years and is still in use today.

Hydrogen gas was first isolated in 1766 by Henry Cavendish, an English scientist.

John Grueber and Albert d'Orville, who were sent by the Pope on a mission to China in 1661, were the first Europeans to reach Lhasa, the capital of Tibet.

Insects were the first animals to fly. They appeared on Earth 300 million years ago and were the only creatures in the air until flying reptiles appeared 195 million years ago.

Ink is first thought to have been used in the third century, when it was used for writing on wooden tablets.

Scientists have made plaster moulds of fossil skulls in an attempt to discover when man first learnt to speak. Early man made primitive sounds, but it seems that the first men capable of making the range of sounds we use in speech today lived between 35,000 and 20,000 years ago.

It is thought that the Earth was first formed about 4,600 million years ago.

Envelopes were not used for letters until 1839. The first letters before this were folded up and sealed with wax, and the address written on the outside.

One of the first structures seen by astronauts as they return from space is the Great Wall of China, the main part of which is 2,150 miles (3,460 kilometres) long, nearly three times the length of Britain.

The practice of putting clocks back and forwards in the autumn and spring to mark the end and start of British Summer Time was first begun in 1925.

The summit of Mount Everest was reached for the first time on the same day as Queen Elizabeth II's coronation.

WATERY FIRSTS

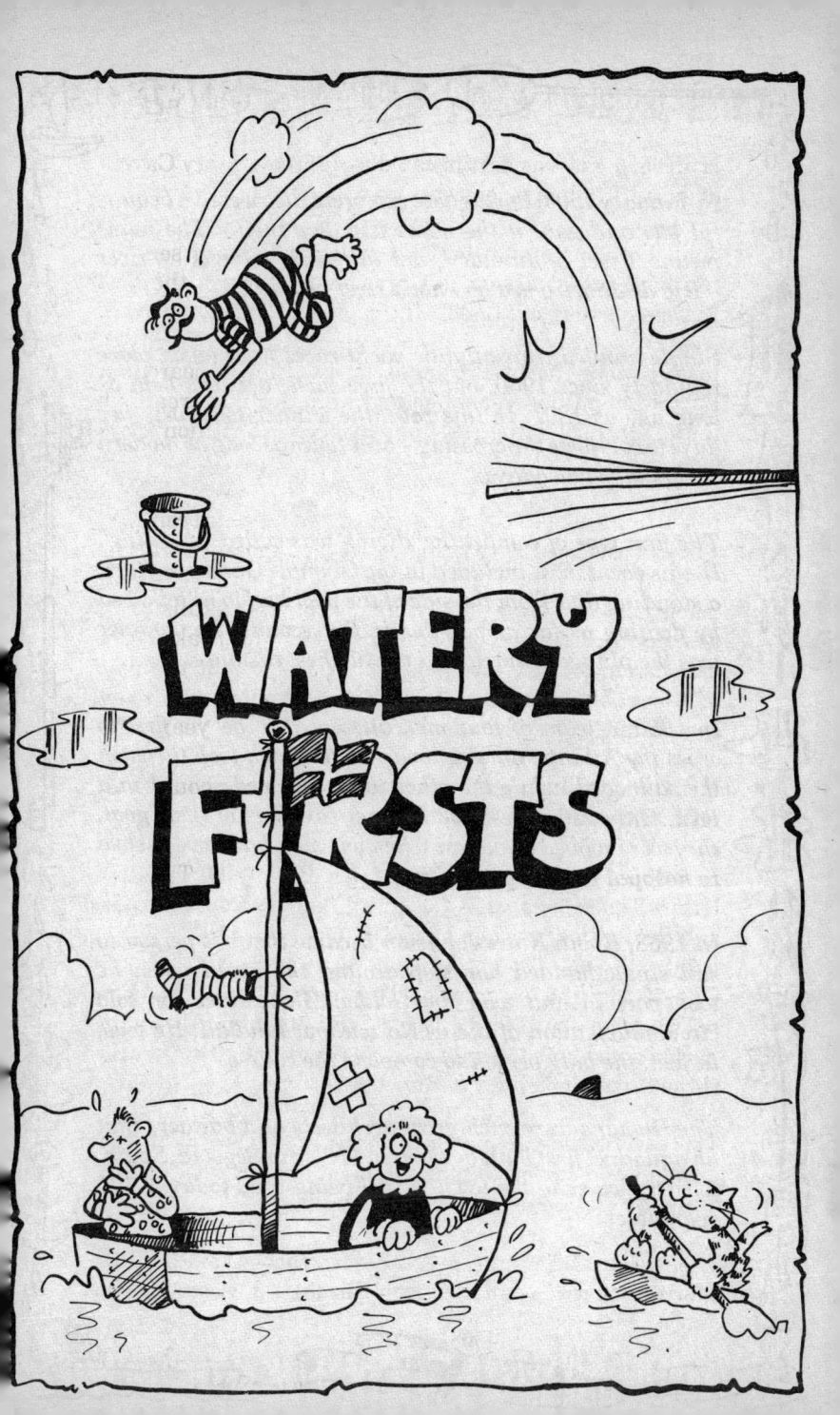

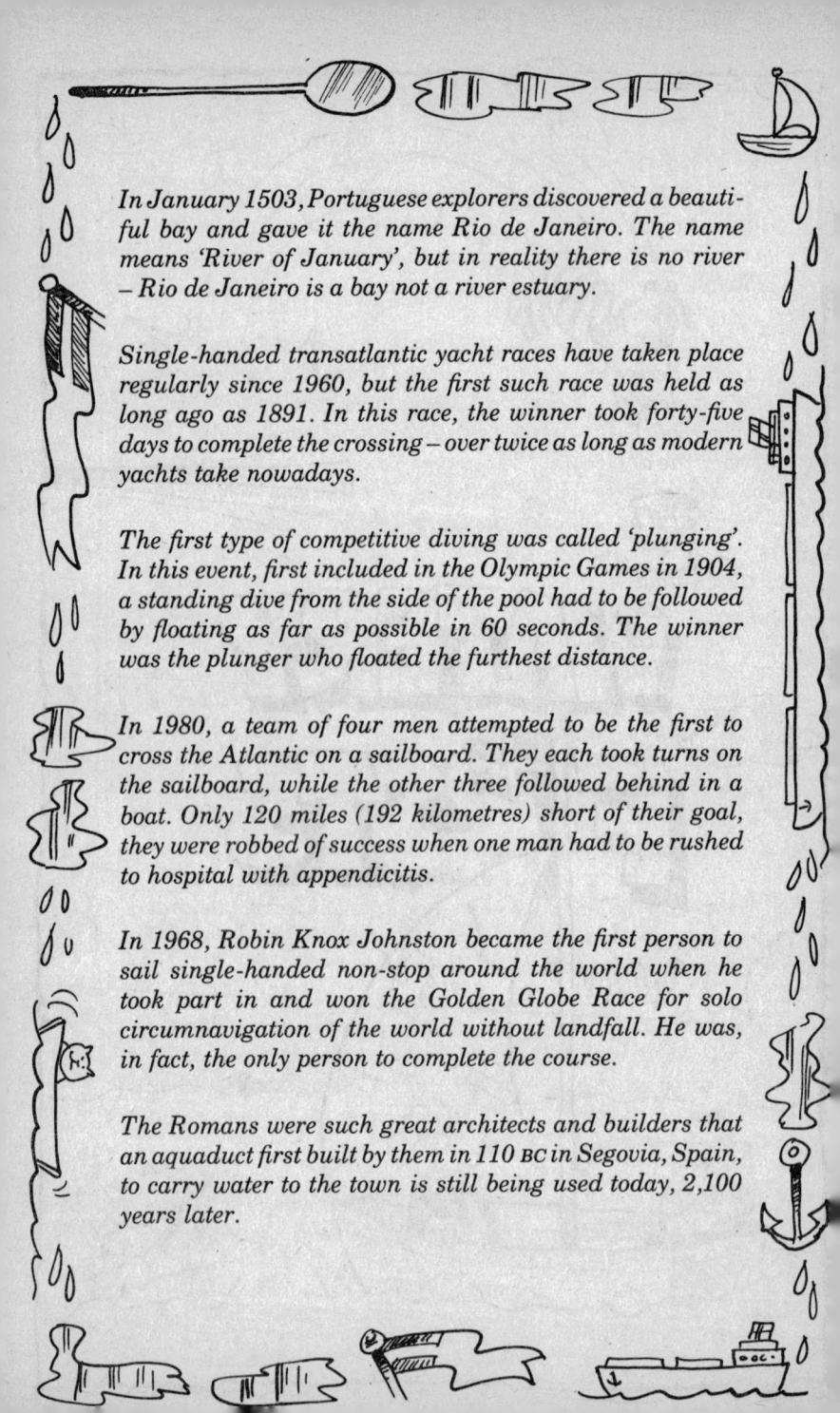

In January 1503, Portuguese explorers discovered a beautiful bay and gave it the name Rio de Janeiro. The name means 'River of January', but in reality there is no river – Rio de Janeiro is a bay not a river estuary.

Single-handed transatlantic yacht races have taken place regularly since 1960, but the first such race was held as long ago as 1891. In this race, the winner took forty-five days to complete the crossing – over twice as long as modern yachts take nowadays.

The first type of competitive diving was called 'plunging'. In this event, first included in the Olympic Games in 1904, a standing dive from the side of the pool had to be followed by floating as far as possible in 60 seconds. The winner was the plunger who floated the furthest distance.

In 1980, a team of four men attempted to be the first to cross the Atlantic on a sailboard. They each took turns on the sailboard, while the other three followed behind in a boat. Only 120 miles (192 kilometres) short of their goal, they were robbed of success when one man had to be rushed to hospital with appendicitis.

In 1968, Robin Knox Johnston became the first person to sail single-handed non-stop around the world when he took part in and won the Golden Globe Race for solo circumnavigation of the world without landfall. He was, in fact, the only person to complete the course.

The Romans were such great architects and builders that an aquaduct first built by them in 110 BC in Segovia, Spain, to carry water to the town is still being used today, 2,100 years later.

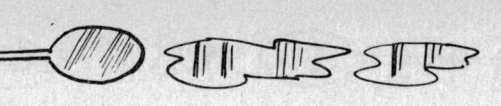

The first boats, made more than 8,000 years ago, were dug-out canoes fashioned from hollowed tree trunks. Remains have been found of one that was 16 metres long, which is a remarkable size for a canoe.

The first submarine was built in 1624. It was the work of a Dutch designer called Cornelius Drebbel and was made of a wooden frame covered with greased leather to keep it waterproof. King James I is said to have gone inside the submarine and to have been taken 15 feet (5 metres) under the surface of the River Thames. The British Admiralty described it as a novelty that would never catch on.

It is an amazing fact that if you sail across the Atlantic Ocean towards the mouth of the great Amazon river on the north-east coast of South America, tasting the sea water at regular intervals, you will first taste fresh water well out at sea long before you sight land. This is because there is such a huge volume of water flowing out from the mighty river that it forces the salty water aside as it swells forward into the Atlantic.

The deepest part of the world's oceans was first pin-pointed in 1951 as being in the Mariana Trench in the Pacific Ocean. A depth of 10,990 metres was measured at that time, although subsequent investigations have recorded a slightly greater depth of 11,034 metres.

The lost sea is the name given to what is reputedly the world's largest underground lake, first discovered in 1905. It is situated 91 metres (291 feet) underground in the Craighead Caverns near Tennessee and measures 1.8 hectares (4½ acres).

The Phoenicians are thought to have been the first to sail around Africa, six hundred years before the birth of Christ.

The first man to be convicted by his fingerprints was caught out when he stole a set of billiard balls – he left a thumbprint on a windowsill that was still wet with a coat of fresh paint.

A tradition first started in Roman times and still maintained today concerns statues of famous men on horseback: riders who died a natural death are depicted on a horse with all four of its feet on the ground, whereas those who died in battle are shown on a horse with one or two hooves in the air.

A greater number of first-born babies are born when the moon is waning (getting smaller) than when it is waxing (getting bigger).

During the fourteenth and fifteenth centuries in England, pins were in such short supply that Parliament was forced to make an order that they could only be bought on the first two days of each year. As a result women saved up all through the year to be able to buy as many pins as possible. This gave rise to the phrase 'pin money', which is still much used today to refer to small sums put aside to buy small, often non-essential items.

The first trumpets were played in ancient Denmark nearly 2,000 years before the birth of Christ.

For the first six or seven months of our lives, we can do something that we are unable to do again at any other point in our lives – we can swallow and breathe at the same time.

In the Bible, the Lord's prayer appears for the first time in Chapter 6 of the Gospel of St Matthew. It also appears further on in the Gospel of St Luke.

Both the Arctic and the Antarctic were free from ice at first and it is only comparatively recently in the Earth's history that they have become the coldest places on Earth.

Rod Laver, the Australian tennis star, was the first player to achieve the Grand Slam on two occasions. He won the men's singles title at Wimbledon, and the American, Australian and French championships in both 1962 and 1969.

The first major building in the world that still exists today is the Great Pyramid of Cheops. For more than thirty centuries it was the world's tallest building, but was finally overtaken by the medieval cathedrals of Europe.

In the nineteenth century the Russian chemist, Dmitri Mendelyeev, first compiled the Periodic Table of Elements which listed all the gases, metals, minerals and liquids then known to science. He had sixty-five entries in the table, but in the hundred or so years since then there have been so many new discoveries that number has risen to over 100.

In 1930 Amy Johnson became the first woman to make a solo flight from England to Australia.

Buckingham Palace, the home of the Royal Family, is so-called because it was first built for the Duke of Buckingham in 1703.

Modern methods of building roads were first begun in the late eighteenth century. Before that time, roads in Europe had not been in as good a condition for over 1,000 years, since the collapse of the Roman Empire.

The cost of the preparations in the five years leading up to the first Moon landing in 1969 amounted to nearly the same as that spent by Americans on make-up and other cosmetics during the same period!

The 'Flying Doctor' service in Australia first went into operation in 1928.

The first wrestling is known to date from 2,700 BC at which time it was practised in Iraq.

In 1958 the first hang-gliders tried out the new sport.

In October 1959 postcodes were introduced for the first time in Britain, in Norwich.

The Seven Wonders of the World were first nominated in the second century BC by Antipater of Sidon. They included the Pyramids of Giza which are in Egypt, and the Temple of Artemis of the Ephesians and the Tomb of King Mausolus of Caria, fragments of both of which can still be seen in Turkey. No trace remains of the other four, which were the Hanging Gardens of Babylon, the statue of Zeus at Olympia, the Colossus of Rhodes statue and the world's earliest lighthouse on the island of Pharos off the coast of Egypt.

In AD 600 the first windmills were in use in Persia.

The first railway line for fare-paying passengers was a 12 kilometre (7½ mile) stretch from Swansea to Oystermouth opened in April 1806. The carriages were pulled by horses!

The invention of the stirrup, rather than of new weapons, marked the first major change in the tactics of early warfare, because it meant that men were more easily able to balance on their horses and so they could concentrate more on the actual fighting.

The first British newspaper colour supplement of the kind that is so popular nowadays was that produced by *The Sunday Times*. Originally called *The Sunday Times Colour Section*, it was first published on 4 February, 1962.

In 1741 the first suspension bridge was built in Britain, over the River Tees.

New Zealand had no snakes at first. Those that are found there now were imported from other countries.

The Iceland Parliament, called the Althing, has been in existence since AD 930. It was the first of the present-day parliaments to be founded.

The first written form of the German language was developed in the eighth century.

In 1870, James Starley in Coventry built the first penny-farthing bicycle, which was the start of modern bicycles, with wire-spoked wheels for lightness. The penny-farthing had a very large front wheel and a very small rear one, which gave it its name: a penny was a large coin and a farthing a very small one.

The first aerial hijack occurred in 1948 when some Chinese seized control of a flying boat travelling to Hong Kong from Macao.

Western visitors were only allowed into Nepal for the first time in 1950.

A lieutenant in the Russian air force was the first pilot to loop-the-loop, though whether he did so deliberately or merely by accident is not known.

The first European language to have a written form was Greek.

In an art competition held in Kansas, USA in 1971 the first prize was won by a young artist called D. James Orang, who went on to become quite a well-known painter. What the judges had not realised at the time was that the artist was in fact an orang-utan called Djakarta Jim!

The first barbed wire was invented in 1867 by Lucien Smith. It was first introduced into Britain by Earl Spencer in Leicestershire in 1880.

The 1st of January may be New Year's Day for many people, but by no means for all. The Chinese celebrate their New Year several weeks later, the Jewish and Muslim New Years are in the autumn, and the Buddhists have their New Year celebrations in March or April.

The expression 'to get the sack', used for being dismissed from a job, was first meant literally. Workmen used always to have their own sack of tools, so if a workman was asked to leave a job, his employer gave him his sack to take away with him.

In 1800 the first battery was invented by Alessandro Volta. In 1801 it was demonstrated to Napoleon.

The 50p piece was the first coin of any country to have a seven-sided shape. Its design shows the seated figure of Britannia, originally a symbol of Roman Britain, which has appeared on coins in the UK for over 300 years.

Henry Ford built his first car in 1896.

Saccharin, which is used to sweeten things instead of sugar, was first discovered in 1879 by a scientist called Fahlberg. Eating his tea one evening after a day in the laboratory, he noticed that his bread had a sweet taste. On realising that this sweetness came from his hands, he rushed back to the laboratory and there found the new compound.

CRIME FIRSTS

THE LONG ARM OF THE LAW

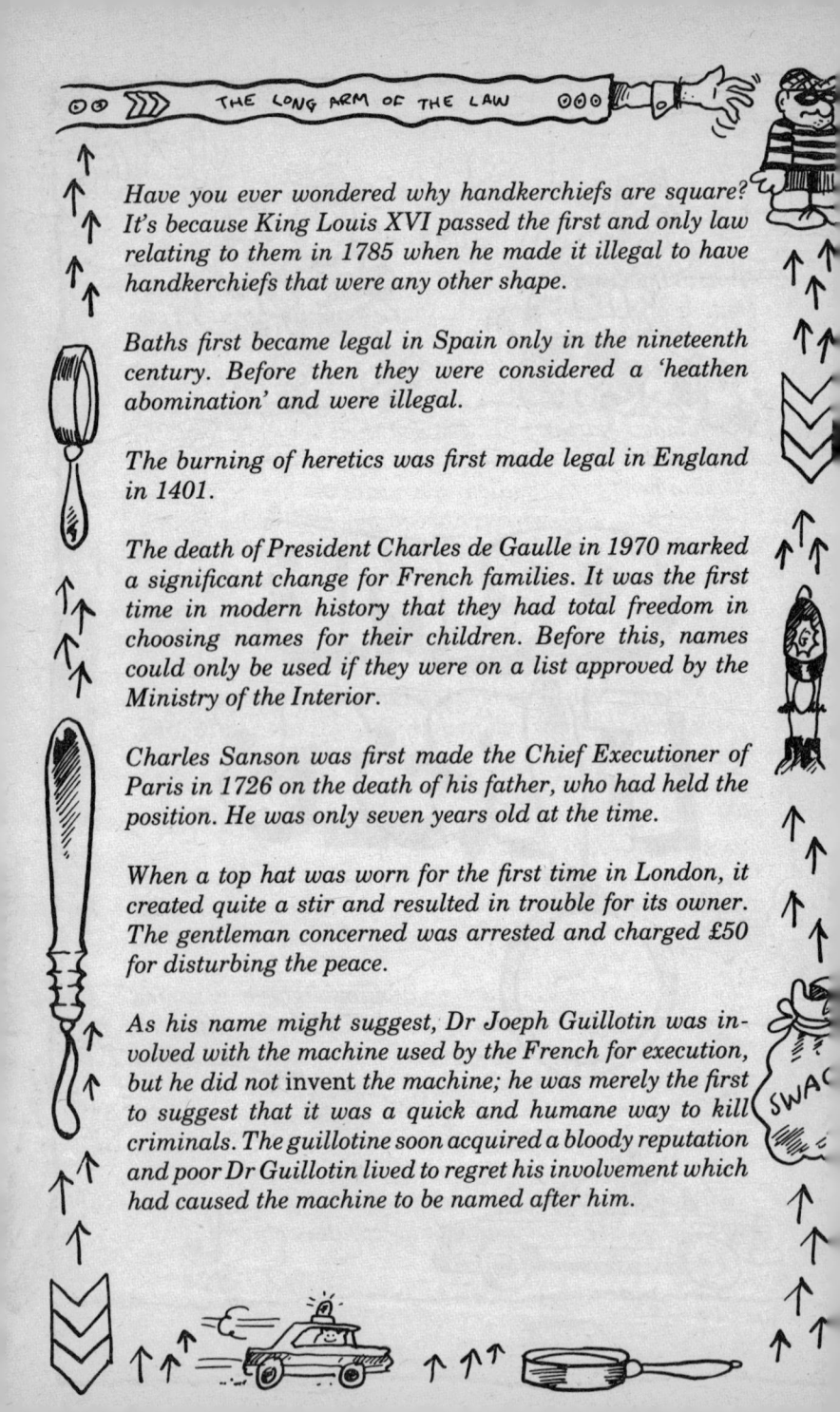

Have you ever wondered why handkerchiefs are square? It's because King Louis XVI passed the first and only law relating to them in 1785 when he made it illegal to have handkerchiefs that were any other shape.

Baths first became legal in Spain only in the nineteenth century. Before then they were considered a 'heathen abomination' and were illegal.

The burning of heretics was first made legal in England in 1401.

The death of President Charles de Gaulle in 1970 marked a significant change for French families. It was the first time in modern history that they had total freedom in choosing names for their children. Before this, names could only be used if they were on a list approved by the Ministry of the Interior.

Charles Sanson was first made the Chief Executioner of Paris in 1726 on the death of his father, who had held the position. He was only seven years old at the time.

When a top hat was worn for the first time in London, it created quite a stir and resulted in trouble for its owner. The gentleman concerned was arrested and charged £50 for disturbing the peace.

As his name might suggest, Dr Joseph Guillotin was involved with the machine used by the French for execution, but he did not invent the machine; he was merely the first to suggest that it was a quick and humane way to kill criminals. The guillotine soon acquired a bloody reputation and poor Dr Guillotin lived to regret his involvement which had caused the machine to be named after him.

THE LONG ARM OF THE LAW

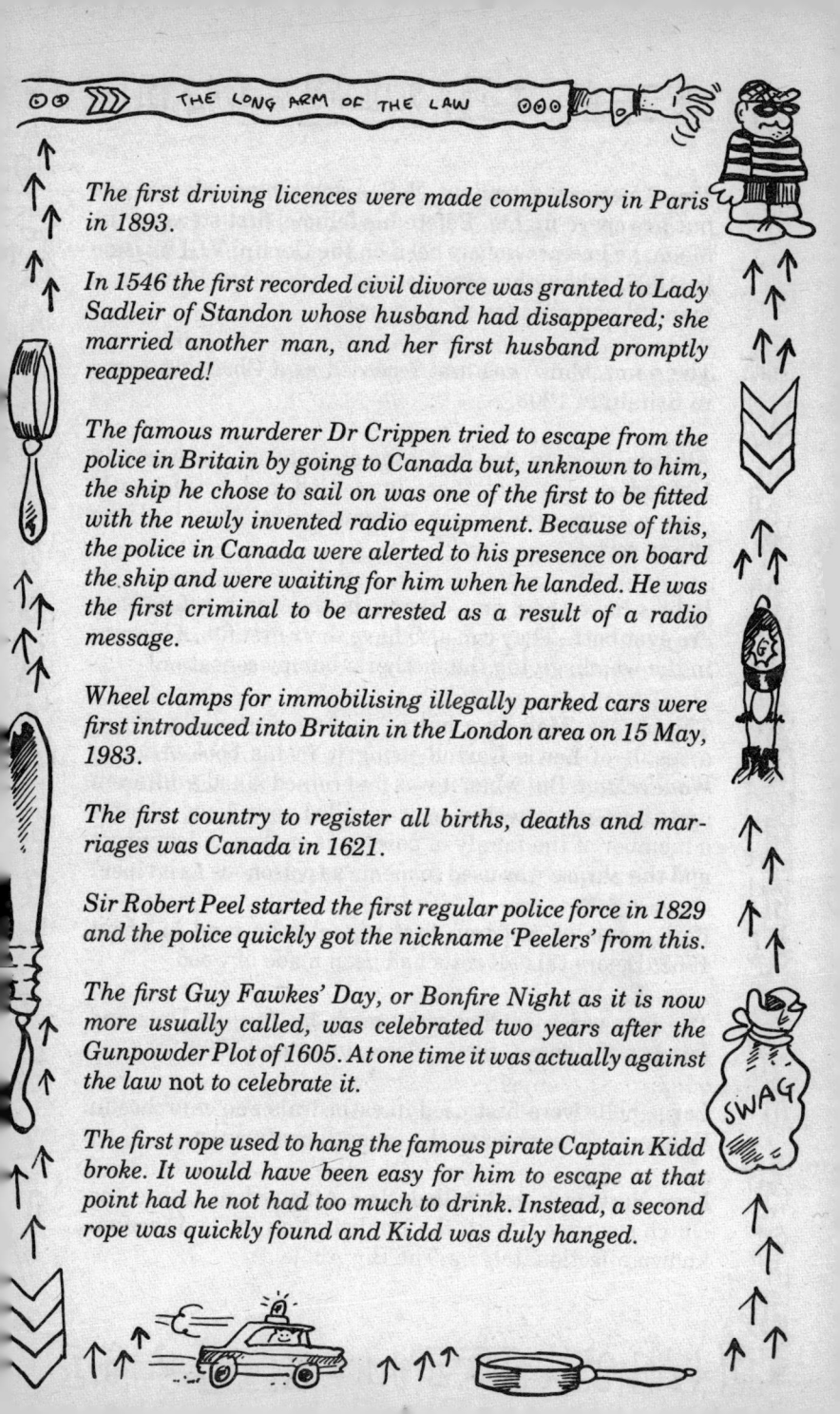

The first driving licences were made compulsory in Paris in 1893.

In 1546 the first recorded civil divorce was granted to Lady Sadleir of Standon whose husband had disappeared; she married another man, and her first husband promptly reappeared!

The famous murderer Dr Crippen tried to escape from the police in Britain by going to Canada but, unknown to him, the ship he chose to sail on was one of the first to be fitted with the newly invented radio equipment. Because of this, the police in Canada were alerted to his presence on board the ship and were waiting for him when he landed. He was the first criminal to be arrested as a result of a radio message.

Wheel clamps for immobilising illegally parked cars were first introduced into Britain in the London area on 15 May, 1983.

The first country to register all births, deaths and marriages was Canada in 1621.

Sir Robert Peel started the first regular police force in 1829 and the police quickly got the nickname 'Peelers' from this.

The first Guy Fawkes' Day, or Bonfire Night as it is now more usually called, was celebrated two years after the Gunpowder Plot of 1605. At one time it was actually against the law not to celebrate it.

The first rope used to hang the famous pirate Captain Kidd broke. It would have been easy for him to escape at that point had he not had too much to drink. Instead, a second rope was quickly found and Kidd was duly hanged.

The American astronaut Neil Armstrong made not one but *two* space flights. Before his famous first steps on the Moon, he had previously been on the Gemini VIII mission in 1966, when the first docking took place between a manned and unmanned spacecraft.

The name Mary was first recorded as a Christian name in Britain in 1203.

Albania became the first atheist state in the world in 1967, declaring that there is no God and consequently closing down every church, mosque and religious building of any sort.

Babies have their first dreams in the womb before they are ever born. They can also have their first fits of hiccups in the womb, giving the mother a bumpy sensation!

The phrase 'Mad as a hatter' was made well-known as a result of Lewis Carroll using it in his book *Alice in Wonderland*. But when it was first coined it had a different meaning – an 'atter' or, as it is called nowadays, adder is a member of the family of poisonous snakes called vipers and the phrase was used to mean 'as poisonous as a viper'.

Rails made of cast-iron first began to be used in about 1768. Before this all rails had been made of wood.

The first wrist-watches were made by Jacquet-Droz and Leschot of Geneva, Switzerland, in around 1790.

Large bells were first used in cathedrals and churches in England as long ago as the seventh century AD.

New York was first called New Amsterdam before the Dutch swapped it with the English. Nowadays it is often known affectionately as 'The Big Apple'.

The worldwide, phenomenally successful McDonald's restaurant chain has its origins in Pasadena, California, USA in 1937 when the two McDonald brothers opened their first-fast food drive-in outlet. They were bought out in 1955 by Ray Kroc, who founded the McDonald's Corporation which now has more than 10,500 outlets around the world selling billions of hamburgers a year.

In 1428 the Earl of Salisbury was the first man to use a cannon in European battle. He also became the first person to be killed by a cannon.

The word 'poacher' comes from the French *poche* meaning pocket and was first coined to refer to men who steal game animals or fish from someone else's land because they usually hide their 'catch' in their pockets. Nowadays you can buy coats with an extra, hidden 'poacher's pocket' in which it is possible to tuck away a great deal!

The first skate-board championships were held in the USA in 1966.

The most famous horse race in England is the Epsom Derby, first run in 1780.

Mistletoe was first used in sacrifices by the Druids of the ancient Celtic civilisation. The romantic tradition of kissing under mistletoe hung up at Christmastime is a much more recent role for this plant, which grows most unromantically as a parasite on trees such as apple.

The idea of paper money was invented by the Chinese. It was first tried out in AD 812 and was in general use by AD 970. The first actual bank-notes were issued in Stockholm, Sweden, in 1661.

In 1858 the first electric burglar alarm was installed in Boston, America.

William Huskisson was a nineteenth-century MP who had a reputation for being accident-prone. At the opening of the first Manchester to Liverpool Railway at which he was present, he rushed across the track to see his friend the Duke of Wellington and became the first person to be run over by a train. A statue was erected in memory of him as a result of this tragic accident.

When the dinosaur called Iguanodon was first discovered in the nineteenth century, palaeontologists (people who study fossils) who tried to assemble the bones that had been found did not get it quite right. They thought that the dinosaur walked on all fours whereas later evidence showed that it tended to walk on only two legs, and they attached an odd spiked bone to the dinosaur's head which was in reality a sharp thumb spike or claw.

The American nickname of 'limey' for a British sailor was first invented when British sailors were issued with lime juice to stop them getting the disease called scurvy which is caused by a lack of vitamin C.

The first inmate of the infamous prison Devil's Island was Alfred Dreyfus.

The girl's name Sarah was not a popular one at first. In its original Hebrew form, spelt *Sarai*, it meant quarrelsome or difficult. Changing the spelling to Sarah gave it the meaning of 'princess' and made the name much more popular!

One of the temples of the Greek goddess of love, Aphrodite, was first discovered by an archaeologist with the very appropriate name of Iris Love.

The first known strike action happened much earlier than you may suppose. In 1160 BC the workers on the tomb of the Pharaoh Rameses III entered into a dispute for more pay because the cost of living had risen.

In the First World War fighting at last died away on the eleventh hour of the eleventh day of the eleventh month of 1918, that is, at 11 a.m. on 11 November, 1918.

The largest chain of chemist shops in the world, Boots The Chemists, had its first outlet in Nottingham, a small shop opened by Jesse Boot.

Hamleys of Regent Street, which is the world's biggest toy shop, was at first situated in Holborn, London when it was founded in 1760. It was not until 1901 that the toy shop moved to its now famous address, Regent Street.

According to Greek mythology, the first crocus flower sprang from the blood of a boy called Crocus, who was playing a game with hoops with the god Mercury when he was killed.

When cakes were first iced the icing was spread on with a bunch of feathers.

Danny Kaye, the famous comedian, was dressed as a water melon seed the first time he appeared on stage.

The *Royal Sovereign*, the first ship armed with 100 cannon, was launched in 1637.

Each wedding anniversary celebrated by married couples is traditionally commemorated by a different substance, some much more expensive than others. Diamonds, gold and silver may be well known to celebrate the sixtieth, fiftieth and twenty-fifth anniversaries respectively, but few people probably know that cotton marks the first anniversary of a marriage.

The first international cricket match was played by Canada and the USA.

Samuel Morse's first career was as an artist working in London in the early 1800s. However, most people will recognise his name in connection with something entirely different – he was the inventor of the Morse Code in 1872.

FEMALE FIRSTS

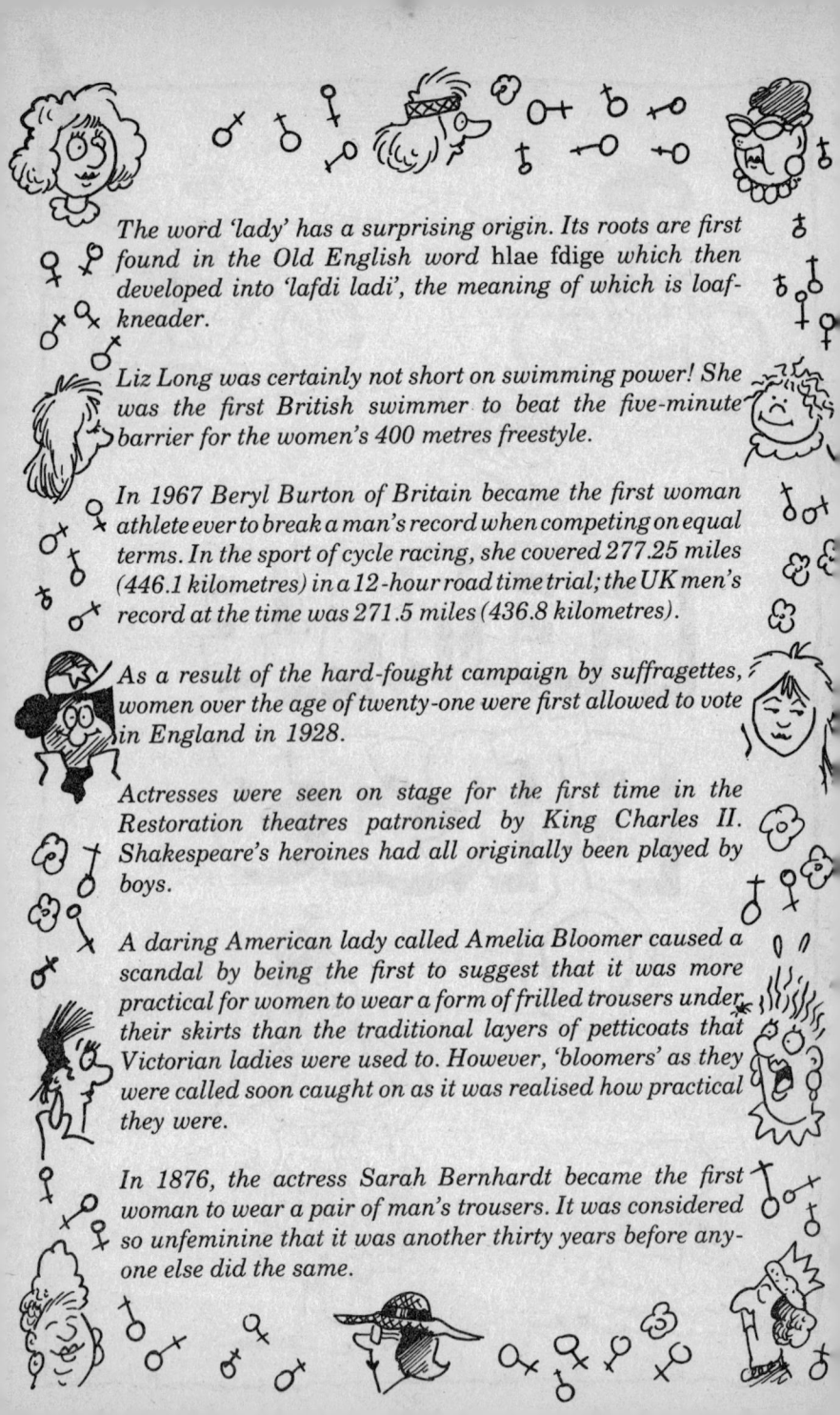

The word 'lady' has a surprising origin. Its roots are first found in the Old English word hlae fdige which then developed into 'lafdi ladi', the meaning of which is loaf-kneader.

Liz Long was certainly not short on swimming power! She was the first British swimmer to beat the five-minute barrier for the women's 400 metres freestyle.

In 1967 Beryl Burton of Britain became the first woman athlete ever to break a man's record when competing on equal terms. In the sport of cycle racing, she covered 277.25 miles (446.1 kilometres) in a 12-hour road time trial; the UK men's record at the time was 271.5 miles (436.8 kilometres).

As a result of the hard-fought campaign by suffragettes, women over the age of twenty-one were first allowed to vote in England in 1928.

Actresses were seen on stage for the first time in the Restoration theatres patronised by King Charles II. Shakespeare's heroines had all originally been played by boys.

A daring American lady called Amelia Bloomer caused a scandal by being the first to suggest that it was more practical for women to wear a form of frilled trousers under their skirts than the traditional layers of petticoats that Victorian ladies were used to. However, 'bloomers' as they were called soon caught on as it was realised how practical they were.

In 1876, the actress Sarah Bernhardt became the first woman to wear a pair of man's trousers. It was considered so unfeminine that it was another thirty years before anyone else did the same.

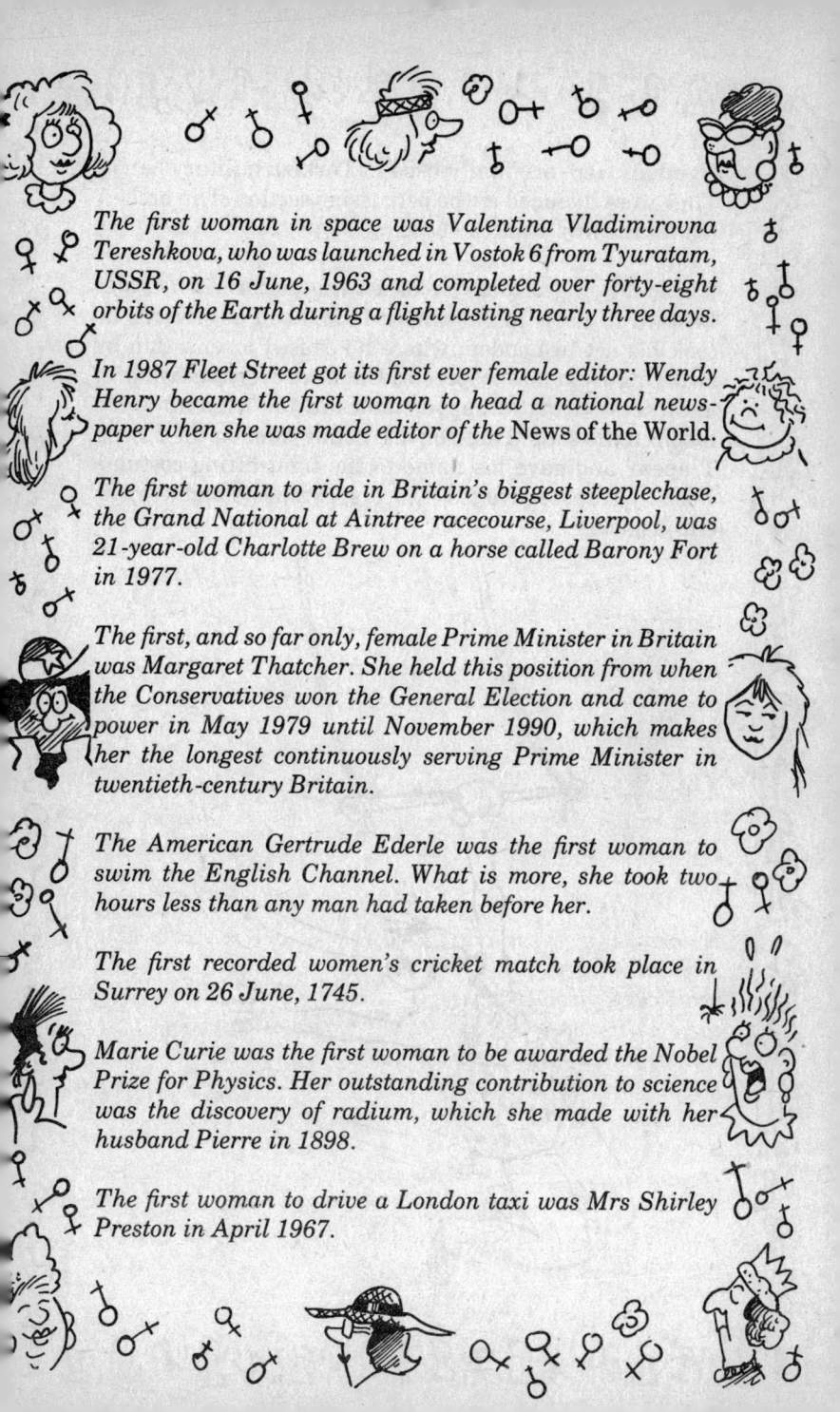

The first woman in space was Valentina Vladimirovna Tereshkova, who was launched in Vostok 6 from Tyuratam, USSR, on 16 June, 1963 and completed over forty-eight orbits of the Earth during a flight lasting nearly three days.

In 1987 Fleet Street got its first ever female editor: Wendy Henry became the first woman to head a national newspaper when she was made editor of the News of the World.

The first woman to ride in Britain's biggest steeplechase, the Grand National at Aintree racecourse, Liverpool, was 21-year-old Charlotte Brew on a horse called Barony Fort in 1977.

The first, and so far only, female Prime Minister in Britain was Margaret Thatcher. She held this position from when the Conservatives won the General Election and came to power in May 1979 until November 1990, which makes her the longest continuously serving Prime Minister in twentieth-century Britain.

The American Gertrude Ederle was the first woman to swim the English Channel. What is more, she took two hours less than any man had taken before her.

The first recorded women's cricket match took place in Surrey on 26 June, 1745.

Marie Curie was the first woman to be awarded the Nobel Prize for Physics. Her outstanding contribution to science was the discovery of radium, which she made with her husband Pierre in 1898.

The first woman to drive a London taxi was Mrs Shirley Preston in April 1967.

Cymbals were originally used in Turkish military bands. They were included in the percussion section of an orchestra for the first time in 1680.

The first flying-trapeze circus act was performed by Jules Leotard in Paris in November 1859. Soon afterwards he took his act to London, where he caused a sensation by swinging from one trapeze to the next over the heads of audiences sitting at supper tables in the Alhambra. He inspired the song 'That Daring Young Man on the Flying Trapeze' and gave his name to the tight-fitting costume worn by trapeze artistes, dancers, gymnasts and keep-fit enthusiasts.

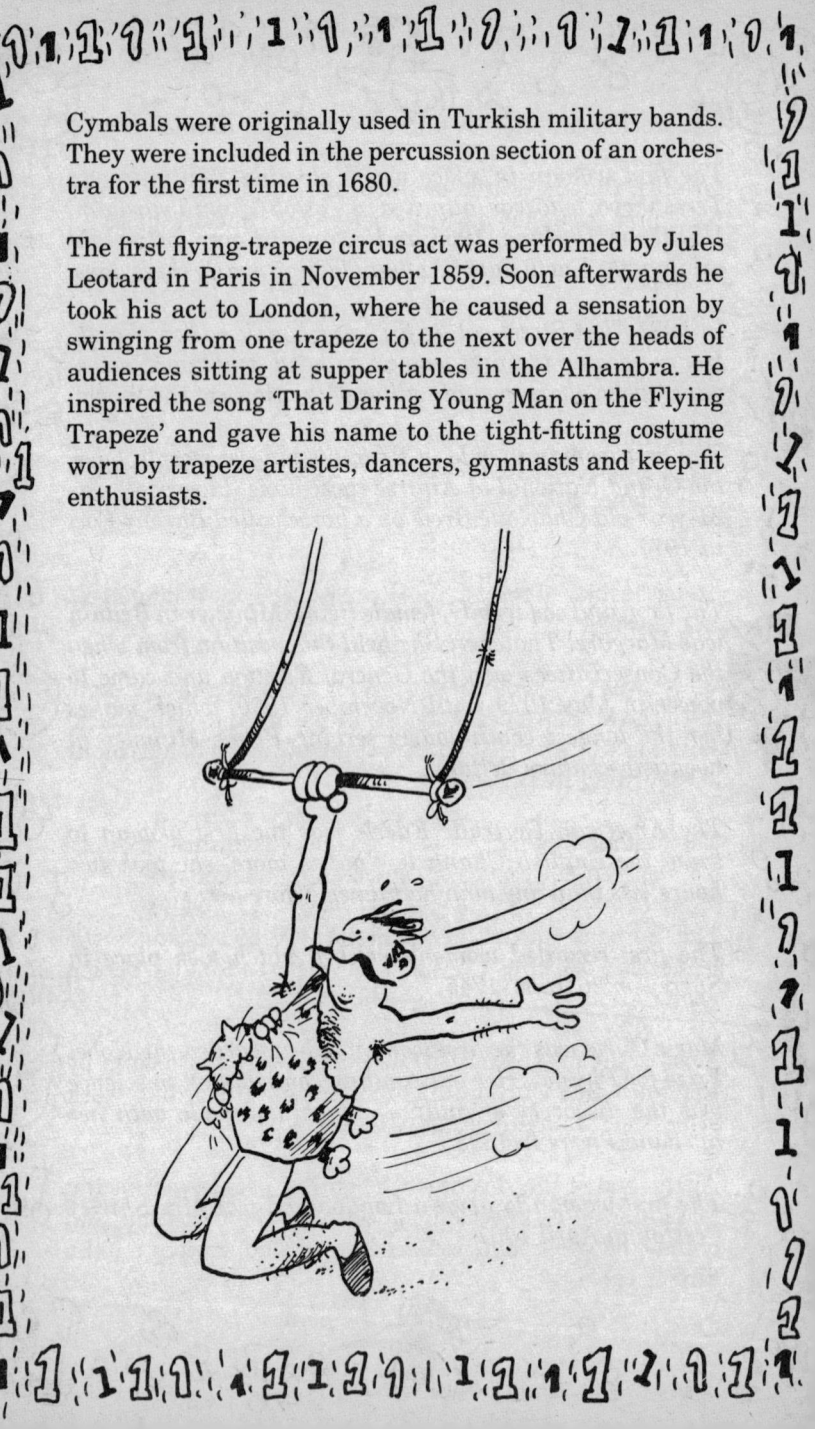

The world's first horror film was *Dr Jekyll and Mr Hyde*.

Graffiti, that is, words or drawings on public buildings, were first scratched on walls before the time of Christ.

Newspaper advertisements first appeared in 1647. The first two printed were quite a contrast! One was for a book published by the clergy of England and the other was for information about the theft of two horses.

After having a sauna, in which you sit and sweat in a very hot, steamy room, the first thing that many people in Finland like to do is to go out and roll about in the snow.

'M' is the first letter of the word 'mother' in most languages in the world.

White was the colour first worn for mourning in England, until the Middle Ages when it became usual to wear black. White is still worn in China, but purple is the usual colour of mourning in Turkey.

The first meaning of the word 'school' was leisure! It comes from the Greek word *schole*, which means leisure.

The Romans first came to Britain in 55 BC under the leadership of Julius Caesar, who was assassinated eleven years later.

Most of the great English cathedrals were first begun by the Normans. Durham has more original Norman work still intact than any other cathedral.

At the end of the seventeenth century people were using forks as well as knives to eat with for the first time, and china and glass had replaced wood and pewter on the dinner table.

Another Knight Book

Phillip Schofield and Pat Kellener

THE ADVENTURES OF
GORDON T GOPHER

Join Gordon T Gopher, star of BBC children's television, and Phillip Schofield, mega star of the same, as they trek around the United Kingdom. Fun and facts all the way, from the beaches of Great Yarmouth to a ghostly encounter at Glamis . . .

Another Knight Book

Gyles Brandreth

MY RECORD BOOK

The pogo bouncing, baked bean picking, wellie-wanging, jolly jelly record book!

How many pairs of socks can *you* put on, one on top of another? Can *you* eat an entire tin of baked beans in 19 minutes using only a cocktail stick? And what exactly *are* the credentials of being a record-breaker?

YOU'D BETTER GET A COPY AT RECORD SPEED AND FIND OUT!

Another Knight Book

Carol Vorderman

DIRTY, LOUD AND BRILLIANT

Bet you can't

* hold a cup with one finger
* light a torch with a lemon
* make a table top hovercraft

With DIRTY, LOUD AND BRILLIANT – you can!

Masses of easy-to-follow mind-boggling experiments using stuff you'll find at home.

Have a Dirty, Loud and Brilliant time!

Another Knight Book

Jeremy Tapscott

THE INTER GALACTIC JOKE BOOK

Are you spaced out or simply astronuts? Yes? Then put on your Apollo-neck jumper and launch yourself up to planet humour with *The Inter Galactic Joke Book*.

To boldly joke, where no man has joked before! Every space joke under the sun, and a whole lot from even further on. Every one guaranteed to put you into orbit. You'll be glad you bought this joke book. In fact, you'll be over the moon.

Another Knight Book

Rolf Harris

YOUR CARTOON TIME

Did you know that you can draw?

Rolf Harris shows you how – clearly and simply – in YOUR CARTOON TIME. Starting with stick figures, he explains how to develop these step-by-step into your own stylish characters, and there are ideas too for how you can use your drawings – as birthday cards, home movies and so on.

Drawing is fun!

All you need is a pencil, paper and Rolf Harris's book – YOUR CARTOON TIME.